ENLIGHTENMENT, LOVE, AND A STING ARE JUST AROUND THE CORNER AND YET SO FAR AWAY. WELCOME TO THE WORLD OF RECKLESS DREAMING! - *Nick David, Screenwriter*

Imagine a game of Strip Chess surrounded everywhere you turn by strip the soul! Michael and Tara use everything including their wits for weapons! Meanwhile, no knowledge of chess is needed to determine who is winning.

Chess masters Tara, 33, and Michael, 34, stage a high stakes match in San Francisco. Michael is an intense "win at any cost" player with his own obsessions. Tara is an embattled singer and Eastern Philosophy buff. As a reformed alcoholic, she leaves a Buddhist monastery on a quest for enlightenment and love. Tara keeps one vital secret from Michael: She has a brain tumor! Not knowing her condition, Michael hires Destiny, who is into the occult, to play mind games on Tara. However, Destiny plans a lot more than a little harm. That's because at this class, Destiny gets a gadget that lets her enter other people's dreams! As Destiny remarks, "What could they charge me with, reckless dreaming?" The artist Madeleine thinks differently. Meanwhile, psychotic "Dream and People Catcher" Dwayne pursues a Tarot card riddle which doesn't bode well for Tara! More conflict brews in the subplot. The cast is pitted against an unscrupulous producer Wesley. All this is yours to enjoy!

Comments from 3 Professional Script Consultants:

Paul Young's clients have included Academy Award Nominees for Best Picture and Best Original Screenplay as well as the Grand Jury Prize at the Cannes Film Festival. Paul wrote that *"Reckless Dreaming has plausibility, substance, focus, resonance, appeal, and emotional power, which helps to create a single film with its own inner layers and complexities."*—Literary & Screenplay Consultants Woodland Hills, CA

"All in all, you've succeeded in writing an interesting erotic film which has intellectual appeal."—Caroline Blair San Francisco, CA

"You have drawn a very creative visual treatment for moving into and out of dream-space and time."—Constance Richardson Mill Valley, CA

Front Cover: Evidence recklessdreaming.com nickdavid.nd@gmail.com

RECKLESS DREAMING

Screenplay by

Nick David

Story by

Nick David & Michael Kameron

authorHOUSE

AuthorHouse™
1663 Liberty Drive
Bloomington, IN 47403
www.authorhouse.com
Phone: 833-262-8899

Published by AuthorHouse 04/22/2024

ISBN: 978-1-4685-0104-9 (sc)
ISBN: 978-1-4685-0103-2 (e)

Library of Congress Control Number: 2011960397

Print information available on the last page.

Any people depicted in stock imagery provided by Getty Images are models, and such images are being used for illustrative purposes only. Certain stock imagery © Getty Images.

This book is printed on acid-free paper.

ACKNOWLEDGMENT

Very special thanks to Mary Ann, Glenda, Rachel, Tyson, Charlie, Elliot, Ilicia, Bob, Donald, Bill, Dan, and Elly for your invaluable help.

And thanks, beyond measure to my wonderful friend, the late Michael Kameron. Your words brought genuine personality to the characters!

AUTHOR NOTES

Nick David was born in San Francisco and grew up in the Bay Area. He acted in high school plays plus college plays at UC Davis and UC Berkeley. After that, Nick performed alongside Robin Williams at the improvisational "Committee Workshop" in San Francisco.

Basically, Nick David has spent time enjoying dozens of books on Eastern and Western philosophy. Nick found the subject of enlightenment particularly interesting. Also, Tarot cards are a significant factor in Reckless Dreaming due to Mr. David's interest in them.

Additionally, his passion for art comes into play. An artist named Madeleine influences multiple events. Plus, Nick is fascinated by the meaning of dreams. In fact, the Copper Star Device in Reckless Dreaming for entering other people's dreams comes from that!

With plenty of heartfelt knowledge, Nick David began writing Reckless Dreaming. He developed daring characters and plot lines over an extensive period. Along the way, Nick sought out and took the best of various professional script critics' advice. Meanwhile, he always maintained his overall vision for the work. That included ensuring that sex and nudity are never gratuitous. Rather, they occur or don't occur based on the plot and character needs.

Furthermore, each spiritual viewpoint must be authentic and represented well. Finally, as a lifetime San Francisco area resident, Nick intimately knows the locations that were chosen.

Thank you so much for your interest!

Chess notation is utilized for continuity in the ongoing game. Meanwhile, the Tarot cards are arranged in story order.

Reckless Dreaming

THE MAGICIAN.

THE EMPRESS.

THE STAR.

ACE of SWORDS.

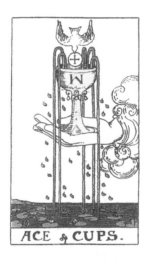

ACE of CUPS.

THE HIGH PRIESTESS

THE FOOL.

THE TOWER.

THE DEVIL.

SCRIPT CODE: EXT. = (EXTERIOR) OUTDOOR SCENE, INT. = (INTERIOR) INDOOR SCENE, O.S. = OFF SCREEN, & V.O. = VOICE OVER.

"RECKLESS DREAMING"

FADE IN:

EXT. OCEAN - DAY

A big boat rumbles along with a well-dressed male PROFESSOR, 43, on board with eight other passengers. MADELEINE, 29, artist, streaked medium length brunette, wears a beret. She stands along with DESTINY, 24, an alluring Asian-American woman who dances to a different drummer.

Meanwhile, the wind and the boat speed up. Some passengers hold onto the rails. A few other voyagers including those mentioned fly away!

INT. AUDITORIUM - DAY

Darkened stage and curtains. With an object in his hand, the professor gets out of a front row chair, struts to a wall, and turns on the lights.

                    PROFESSOR
        Okay, class, please come back from this daydream.

About fifteen people, including all eight from the boat, shift straighter from a slumped position in their desk chairs. Destiny and Madeleine are sitting next to each other.

Maroon velvet pouches are scattered about the seats. Each student's desktop contains a typed page and a gleaming five-point copper star. The hollow star center holds an oblong quartz crystal. The professor resides stage front.

                    PROFESSOR
          Congratulations to all who joined me on this
          fast boat ride. Plus, some of you did focus on
          your hands and took flight!

Eight people including Destiny and Madeleine stand up, clap, and cheer before sitting back down.

                    PROFESSOR
          The rest of you -- don't worry. It's much easier
          to enter someone else's dream during actual
          sleep when you're deeper into the subconscious.
          You can try for a specific friend or lover but
          don't be surprised if you encounter the world
          of a stranger.

The professor raises the shiny star.

                    PROFESSOR
          Copper and quartz crystal are a powerful
          electrical energy combination. These two ancient
          forces vibrate in harmony.

He touches the crystal and a copper point on the gadget.

                    PROFESSOR
          They transmit; you receive. Just follow the
          instructions. This is not just a dream catcher;
          it's also a "people catcher".

                    MADELEINE
                 (bites her nails)
          Geez!

Destiny rubs the star across her chest.

                              DESTINY
              This is a nuclear weapon!

                             MADELEINE
              Only if you use it that way, Destiny.

                             PROFESSOR
              Dream interaction is a skill you can own for a
              lifetime. The device is excellent especially if
              you supply concentration.

The whole class pays rapt attention.

                             PROFESSOR
              This is a new dimension in human communication.
              If you enter the subconscious of another person
              deeply enough, you can even affect what they do
              when they're awake!

EXT. HOSPITAL - DAY (RAIN)

A steady downpour drenches snarled vehicles. TARA, 33, a striking,
intelligent woman with shaved hair, exits the hospital. She pulls
a bottle of Scotch from her coat pocket and takes a couple of
long swigs before putting it back.

                                                      DISSOLVE TO:

EXT. BUDDHIST MONASTERY - DAY

A large Buddha statue dwells in front of a rustic abode in the
woods.

INT. TARA'S ROOM AT THE MONASTERY - DAY

Tara, shift dress and hair now short, sits at the computer.
Display: "POSSIBLE $500,000 WINNER TAKES ALL CHESS INSTITUTE
MATCH BETWEEN MICHAEL MCALLISTER AND TARA SILVER."

A bed and shelved books. Small chess set and ornate cup on a
side table. A labyrinth featured on the wall.

Tara's fingers caress a worn notebook hand-titled "KEYS TO THE CASTLE." Her hand movement stops.

                                        DISSOLVE TO:

INT. COTTAGE - FATHER'S LIVING ROOM - DAY

Little girl on a man's lap. His neat clothes and British accent suit each other. Fully set chess game. He lifts the knight.

                        FATHER
        The horse can jump over anything that gets in
        its way.

                        CHILD
        I want to go for a ride!

INT. BUDDHIST MONASTERY - DAY

Brother Robert, 42, a dark-haired, stern-looking man attired in a traditional monk's robe, stands behind Tara. He carries a small stick. Tara's eyes remain shut. Brother Robert rouses her with his free hand.

                        TARA
        Oh.
        He flicks his stick.

                        BROTHER ROBERT
        Most students would get a whack. Two years here
        should have taught you that daydreaming is no
        substitute for meditation.

                        TARA
        I decided against accepting the offer, Brother
        Robert.

                        BROTHER ROBERT
        What?

Tara rises to face the monk.

> TARA

Money was set aside by the Chess Institute for a match my father never got to play. Turns out his opponent's son in San Francisco is issuing me an official challenge.

> BROTHER ROBERT

The computer is for the study of religious documents only.

She glides her hand across the screen.

> TARA

I branched out.

Brother Robert raises his stick, then lowers it.

> BROTHER ROBERT

I can't.

> TARA

No one can... anymore.

> BROTHER ROBERT

What do you expect, Tara?

> TARA

To still be treated like everyone else.

> BROTHER ROBERT

Please understand; it changes things when a tumor could kill you at any time.

> TARA

I need to accept that. So, is it better to bury these with me or give them away?

Tara picks up the cup.

> TARA

The chess trophy my father never pawned and...

Tara touches "KEYS TO THE CASTLE."

                    TARA
Found at his side dedicated to me. If I had
my health, I would win the match for him and
establish a charity in his name.

                BROTHER ROBERT
Spiritual books will help you cope with everything
you're facing.

                    TARA
Odd word -- cope. But that's the future --
coping with nausea, losing balance, worse and
worse headaches.

Tara presses the chess cup and notebook against the sides of her
head. She appears lost in thought before suddenly returning the
two objects to their original places. Tara turns to the monk.

                    TARA
No, it doesn't have to be that way! I can take
on Michael and the symptoms too.

                BROTHER ROBERT
You have enough challenges so why take on
chess? It's war; it's a battle of egos and you
could easily give in to temptation.

                    TARA
I'm over that.

                BROTHER ROBERT
The path to the universal mind is full of
thorns.

She grasps the back of her head.

                    TARA
Then, this thorn can help me find enlightenment
before my death.

She strokes the monitor.

> TARA

And how rough could anything else be if I'm with Michael? He writes me in poetry.

> BROTHER ROBERT

I look for silver linings, but I can't seem to --

> TARA

How about this? A whole new place filled with people who don't know about my illness. It's just what the doctor ordered.

> BROTHER ROBERT

Keep drinking your tea. You never know.

They hug.

> TARA

I want to go out in a blaze of glory, not a world of pity!

EXT. SAN FRANCISCO - LAND'S END BEACH - DAY

MICHAEL, 34, top collar buttoned conservatively dressed type, is an ego-driven bookworm with his own obsessions. Madeleine, fresh beret employed, faces the sea from behind an easel. She paints while Michael, perched on a rock, reads. He looks her way.

> MICHAEL

I'll buy this one too, Madeleine. I love the ocean.

> MADELEINE

Um... sold! It's yours.

> MICHAEL

And it doesn't have to be a complete surprise --
I'm curious.

He wanders over to the painting. It depicts trees and active factory smokestacks that blend into each other along a spiraling path.

MICHAEL
Maybe, you could attach a note -- inspired by...

He gestures toward the water.

MADELEINE
(smiles)
You could inspire me with a kiss, Michael.

She reaches for Michael, but he moves away.

MICHAEL
I still have some baggage.

MADELEINE
Ask me if I care.

INT. DION AND LOLA'S BEDROOM - DAY

Indian SITAR music pervades the luxurious setting. Incense and candles burn on a nightstand.

Bedecked in a lounging robe, DION, 32, enters holding a sheath-enclosed sword with a heavily jeweled handle. Dreadlocks, facial piercings, and earrings -- Dion is rough around the edges. Robed as well, LOLA, 28, sometimes a free spirit, entices with her long blond hair and standard Southern accent.

She is kneeling on a king-size bed replete with brass canopy. Dion pulls the sword out. He performs a short benediction of sacred love. On the wall, a yin-yang symbol glistens.

DION
Are they melting together or drifting apart today? It's always a trip, Lola.

A statue of a warrior rules the other nightstand.

LOLA
I vote for opposites melting together. Yes!

A return to the bed reveals Lola and Dion entwined nude in the upright lotus position. Their stillness breaks when Dion gives Lola a couple of hard spankings on her buttocks.

                    LOLA
        Ooh, Dion!

INT. MICHAEL'S BATHROOM - DAY

                    MICHAEL
        He stands near the toilet bowl.

Personal interview, take one. I love acting and I love writing about stuff I would never dare to do. I should tell you my motto: Whatever I can imagine is an extension of myself. Wesley, I must also tell you something; I hate like hell not being paid. I'm being taken advantage of and it's sickening! There, I've said it, at least to myself.

INT. MOVING TRAIN - COMPARTMENT - DAY

Chess trophy and "KEYS" notebook on a table. During the VOICE OVER, Tara, pawn in hand, closes it in her fist, turns her fist down, and waves her other hand over the proceedings.

                    FATHER (V.O.)
        Every piece in chess is more powerful than
        the single pawn. Yet it is only this meek
        single pawn which possesses the supreme power
        of transformation.

Tara turns her closed hand up again. She opens it to disclose a queen in place of a pawn.

                    TARA
                    (smiles)
        I'll always be your Little Magician.

She places the noble lady down and opens the notebook. Pastoral scenery rolls by during the VOICE OVER.

                          FATHER (V.O.)
          The Good Book puts nirvana this way: The meek
          shall inherit the earth and shall delight
          themselves in the abundance of peace. Please
          keep this passage about results in mind.

EXT. SAN FRANCISCO - 48TH AVE. - MICHAEL'S HOUSE - DAY

Beach and waves form background against the adjacent highway. A
beach tunnel looms across the street. A flight of stairs gains
entrance to this two-story residence.

INT. MICHAEL'S LIVING ROOM - DAY

A fancy, large, and messy room complete with fireplace is a
landmine of newspapers, magazines, book piles, trophies, and
bookcases filled to overflowing. A computer station oversees
the chaos.

A collection of small clocks and two white candles in glass
holders inhabit a shelf next to a carved mirror.

Carrying the book "FREE YOUR MIND", Michael plops himself into
one of two large club chairs. The square end table between
them holds a basic chess set, chess clock, and "CHESS MASTER"
magazine. Michael opens to a bookmarked page.

                          MICHAEL
                       (reads audibly)
          "What we feel when we're awake, we can see while
          sleeping. So, angels are the very real stuff
          from which dreams are made."

Wall-hung painting: A large black and white abstract resembles
an ink blot.

                          MIMI (O.S.)
          You're a complete asshole!

Another painting depicts white rain against a darkened sky
interspersed with various animals.

                            MICHAEL
                          (reads aloud)
          "Anyone noticing the slightest imperfection,
          please report directly to God."

                            MIMI (O.S.)
          She even has a nickname. How God damned cute!

Michael hovers next to a far wall where a pair of clocks tell
somewhat different stories.

                            MICHAEL
          Identical in every way but they keep separate
          times. It's crazy.

He checks his watch, adjusts the clocks to match, and talks while
returning to his chair.

                            MICHAEL
          Okay, half an hour, no interruptions.

Michael opens "CHESS MASTER" magazine. The silence breaks fast
as MIMI, 29, a fashionable loudmouth outfitted in high heel shoes
and slip, thunders in. She carries a small open box of printed
material.

                            MIMI
          You have a very subtle way of telling me another
          woman is taking my place!

The article from which Michael glances up could have been titled
"Calm before the Storm."

                            MICHAEL
          Put those back, Mimi. They're private.

                            MIMI
          Right! I practically tripped over them.

She places the box on a table and grabs the top letter.

                              MIMI
          "Dear Tara, Time apart is time wasted. Come meet
          me over the horizon and under the rainbow." Oh,
          my Gawd!

She stuffs the letter back into the box.

                              MIMI
          This is the same crap you wrote me. What a con
          artist!

With the magazine table-bound, Michael points at her shoes.

                            MICHAEL
          Those spectator pumps would go well with your
          black satin dress.

                              MIMI
          How can you think about my high heels at a time
          like this?

She waves her arm around.

                              MIMI
          All these nutty books have taught you nothing,
          Michael.

                            MICHAEL
          They let me explore the possibilities.

                              MIMI
          What the hell for? I don't have to analyze my
          life to death. I'm just trying to get through it!

Michael raises "CHESS MASTER" magazine for a moment.

                            MICHAEL
          Tara has been improving her chess skills at the
          monastery. So, I can't rely on her to make dumb
          moves unless you count giving all the money to
          charity if she wins.

MIMI

That is dumb.

MICHAEL

Anyway, she arrives tomorrow morning for our match and I've offered to let her stay here.

Mimi puts the box down.

MIMI

Are you insane? What do you plan to do, screw her under my nose!?

MICHAEL

Let's not fight. My thirtieth win in a row against another grandmaster sets a modern record. So, I need to learn about Tara and exploit all her weaknesses!

He rises to pat a stack of nearby books.

MICHAEL

Victory assures a book deal and my place in history.

MIMI

If it's such a big event, where are all the reporters?

MICHAEL

They're always prying into personal affairs, so Tara and I will just keep them informed. Why don't you concentrate more on your own life? Be your own person.

Mimi shifts into hands on hips mode and glares at Michael.

MIMI

Be my own person, be one hundred percent me. Okay, I will light up when and where I want.

Mimi gets a cigarette to her lips before Michael swats it away.

                    MICHAEL
          Outside only -- you know how allergic I am.

Mimi storms over to Michael's chess set.

                     MIMI
          Okay, a little less than one hundred percent me
          but still my own person -- your stupid games
          are ruining my life!

She uses her arm to wipe most of the chess pieces off the table!
The Calm after the Storm points at the board.

                    MICHAEL
          You shouldn't have done that, Mimi. You've left
          your position completely exposed.

                     MIMI
          My sister was right! Boys who read too much make
          lousy lovers. And that one's totally true! Now
          it's your move; either call off this contest and
          this bitch or I'm out of here!

EXT. SAN FRANCISCO - WAX MUSEUM - NIGHT

An eerie glow lights up the building. A few life-sized wax figures
guard the premises. The ticket booth holds Destiny, replete with
nose rings and black outfit. Michael strolls up and presents her
with a medium-size manila envelope.

                    MICHAEL
          It's all there, Destiny, along with the picture
          and biography you requested. I don't want to
          know.

                    DESTINY
          Of course.

She briefly pulls a thin stack of one hundred dollar bills out
of the envelope.

                         MICHAEL
I only raised five hundred. Anyway, I could win
without your help.

                         DESTINY
Of course.

                         MICHAEL
Our transaction must remain a secret from all
parties.

                         DESTINY
Of course.

                         MICHAEL
Use mind games only; you shouldn't do any
physical harm to our "Little Magician."

                         DESTINY
Now, you're taking all the fun out of it. So...
how about a free admission?

                         MICHAEL
No, I feel like I'm already in there.

                         DESTINY
It could include some extra thrills.

                         MICHAEL
Maybe later, in celebration.

She lifts the envelope.

                         DESTINY
Meanwhile, I'll be pleasuring you in other ways.

INT. MICHAEL'S LIVING ROOM - DAY

Michael tidies up while armed with paraphernalia. He kicks open
the coat closet. A half-dozen assorted high heel shoes fall from
a high shelf. A teddy bear follows in close pursuit. Michael
attempts to pick up but that causes him to drop everything he's
holding!

                         MICHAEL
          Damn it!

INT. MICHAEL'S LIVING ROOM - DAY

A medieval chess set has replaced the basic set on the end table.
Plus, no chess clock. The fallen high heel shoes and teddy bear
remain in place amidst the debris.

With a large antique suitcase next to her, Tara, simple outfit
with scarf, runs her fingers past a couple of books on the
shelves.

                         TARA
          Physics and religion, interesting bedfellows.

                         MICHAEL
          Nah. Psychology would be more fun in the bedroom.

The pile of high heel shoes.

                         TARA
          I presume Mimi left these?

Michael rummages through them.

                         MICHAEL
          Wow! It's always something. She left her best
          mules and she's certain to miss these stiletto
          heels.

                         TARA
          Will you miss her as well?

He lifts the teddy bear.

                         MICHAEL
          We had a great relationship from her shoes on
          down.

Michael places the stuffed animal on a chair.

                    MICHAEL
Most times, things only work out in dreams.

Tara notices the medieval chess set.

                    TARA
Oh, how beautiful!

                    MICHAEL
I use it for special occasions.

                    TARA
I feel privileged.

                    MICHAEL
The set once belonged to the great chess legend,
Paul Morphy.

                    TARA
Didn't Morphy die in some strange way?

Michael shudders and changes the subject.

                    MICHAEL
My friend Madeleine... that's one of hers.

The black and white abstract painting.

                    TARA
It looks like a Rorschach test. What's the title?

                    MICHAEL
Who knows? She never names anything. Anyway,
there's a room available where Madeleine and
her friend Destiny live; I've set it up for you
to stay there.

Tara picks up the black knight from the board. Michael grabs
it - the knight scratches her hand.

                    TARA
Ow!

Michael puts the piece back. Tara spots a shelf-bound picture of Michael and Mimi.

                    TARA
        So where's the photo of me you requested?

                    MICHAEL
        Let's get started.

The chess clock on the mantle.

                    TARA
        Does playing one game without any time limits
        for five hundred thousand dollars make you
        nervous?

                    Michael
        I do have home field advantage.

Michael brings his hands out from behind his back, fists closed. Tara chooses a hand containing a black pawn. She puts the piece back in place while Michael does the same with the white pawn in his other hand.

                    TARA
        I would like to dedicate this game to our --

                    MICHAEL
        May the best player win!

He pushes his king's pawn out two spaces to begin the game. Then in rather quick mode: 1 Black P-K4 2 White Kt-KB3 Black Kt-QB3 3 White B-B4 Black Kt-B 4 White Kt-Kt5 Black P-Q4.

EXT. GOLDEN GATE PARK - CONSERVATORY OF FLOWERS - DAY

An expansive lawn and flower garden in front of a colossal glass mansion. The sidewalk bordering the greenery finds ruffle-shirted, cavalier DWAYNE, 28.

He saunters alongside JASMINE, a leashed, hirsute Shih-Tzu with large brown eyes. Dwayne's free arm animates through the air as he converses with his dog.

                        DWAYNE
        You follow your scent, girl. I follow my dreams.
        No conflict! Just know this, Jasmine. Dwayne
        only kills for a higher cause!

EXT. HIGHWAY 1 - NORTHBOUND - SPORTS CAR (MOVING) - DAY

 With the ocean to the driver's left, a sleek machine tools along.

INT. SPORTS CAR (MOVING) - DAY

Southern Belle Lola in a flowery dress. Her gorgeous passenger
JUNE, African American, 29, enjoys the unexpected more than she
admits. She wears a short skirt.

                        JUNE
        It's so nice to get out, to show off a little.
        With Quentin, I don't know... there's nothing...
        very exciting.

                        LOLA
                     (driving)
        That's why we have the circle. People share
        their secrets, indulge their desires.

                        JUNE
        I love Quentin, so I have certain limits. After
        all, we're married.

                        LOLA
        How about that one little fantasy we discussed?

                        JUNE
        Well, I have been trying to dare myself.

A few moments later, June slides her panties off.

                        JUNE
        One, two, buckle my shoe.

                        LOLA
        Wow, that shoe store guy will be getting
        doubly hot!

INT. HAIR AND MAKE-UP TRAILER - DAY

Tara is around mirrors, ingredients for camouflage, brushes, blow dryers, and styling gels.

                    TARA
          Sure, record my opinion, Michael. You and I
          don't get any money for our script; no one gets
          anything for their acting -- it's bullshit!

                    MICHAEL
          I did get a dollar, Tara. That's what I signed
          off for so Wesley could use my house as a
          location.

Tara grasps a jar of make-up.

                    TARA
          This producer treats all the females as pussies,
          if you know what I mean.

She opens it.

                    MICHAEL
          Plus, Wesley is great at stretching truth into
          lies! Meanwhile, I stretch... for my next house
          payment. C'est la vie.

                    TARA
                (opens her arms)
          The marquee -- "now starving in this movie!"

The mirror catches Michael.

                    MICHAEL
          All this hassling for money -- what a rat race.
          Say something, anything to cheer me up.

                    TARA
          My Mom would have been proud of our writing.
          She fought cancer so hard.

Tara sends a handful of powder flying.

                         TARA
        Anyway, how far can you take imagination before
        the line with reality gets...

                         MICHAEL
        ... blurred?

Tara screws the lid back on.

                         TARA
        Everything's a scene. Then I go home at night
        and there isn't much...

                         MICHAEL
        ... dialogue.

                         TARA
        You read my thoughts.
                    (smiles)

That could be dangerous.

INT. DION'S LIVING ROOM - DAY

The jeweled sword occupies its sheath on a wall rack. The
expansive, lavishly furnished room includes a cedar chest and
Dion in a flowing robe.

Smoking a dangling cigarette, Dion experiments with a tune on
the keyboards. He uses the cigarette to light up a joint.

EXT. GOLDEN GATE PARK - THE BANDSHELL - DAY

With Jasmine in tow, Dwayne rambles out of the tunnel. Owner
and dog progress toward the Bandshell.

                         DWAYNE
        Nothing for you to retrieve right now.

Jasmine stares out.

                         DWAYNE
          Why couldn't my aunt have given me a normal
          hunting dog?

A couple of people exchange funny glances.

EXT. GOLDEN GATE PARK - DAY

Under a tree, Lola sits in lotus position. She stares upward for
a moment before fixing her gaze forward.

EXT. DESTINY AND MADELEINE'S FLAT - DAY

An older San Francisco Victorian.

INT. DESTINY'S ROOM - DAY

Black magic decor: masks, skulls, and glass bottles filled with
powder. Funky furniture. Destiny sports a stylish, form-fitting
outfit. She cradles some vines over to a sun-lit bureau. They
share the bureau top with a cut-out newspaper article entitled
"This Sword May Point to the Grail" By Quentin Williams.
Subheading: "Ancient Artifact Worth a Fortune."

Destiny at her desk -- so is a lit votive candle. It props up
The Magician Tarot card (roses and lilies enclose a robed youth
who points a wand skyward from behind a symbol-filled table).

                       PROFESSOR (V.O.)
          If you enter the subconscious of another person
          deeply enough, you can even affect what they do
          when they're awake!

Destiny raises her hand; rings sparkle. Thumb and forefinger
play with melting wax.

                         DESTINY
          If someone I've never met damages Tara beyond
          repair -- that would just be an unfortunate
          accident.

She giggles and pinches out the flame.

EXT. BLUE HERON LAKE ABOVE THE WATERFALL - DAY

Dwayne and an unleashed Jasmine ascend steep stairs beside the
waterfall and shrubbery in Golden Gate Park. San Francisco comes
alive in panoramic view.

                    DWAYNE
          Why did my dream last night take us here,
          Jasmine? Dwayne pulls five Tarot cards from his
          shirt pocket. All Dwayne must do is solve the
          Tarot riddle from his dream.

Dwayne places the cards one at a time across a flat rock as he
mentions them.

The Empress depicts a scepter-holding queen seated in a field.
She wears a fruit-patterned robe and a crown of twelve stars.
The Star shows a naked female under the stars. She pours water
out of two vases.

The Ace of Swords (a hand protruding from a cloud holds a sword
which pierces a crown) comes next. The Magician and the Ace of
Cups (a dove carrying a wafer descends into a grail from which
five streams of water cascade onto a lily pond) complete the
layout.

                    DWAYNE
          When the Empress turns into a Star, the Ace of
          Swords forces the Magician to reveal the Holy
          Grail. That elusive treasure cup will bring
          maximum glory to Dwayne!

Dwayne finds a hand mirror on the ground and picks it up briefly.
Jasmine sniffs around in a small pile of garbage. Dwayne searches
through a few discarded paper bags and old food items. Jasmine
cocks her head as Dwayne talks to her.

                    DWAYNE
          Nothing here but I'm no failure, just because
          I didn't choose the military like my parents.

Dwayne salutes.

DWAYNE

It wasn't in the cards! Meanwhile, Dwayne takes
his medicine just like the next guy when the
mission fails.

Dwayne stands next to the cards.

DWAYNE

First, this quest for the Holy Grail belongs in
only one place -- the history books! I will, yes
you will, toss these fuckin' fates to the wind!

Dwayne picks up the five cards and throws them skyward. They
disperse miles short of a billowing cloud.

In Dwayne's right hand, a dart poises above its intended
victim -- his outstretched left hand. Dwayne stabs the point
into the fleshy part of his left palm! Blood oozes!

DWAYNE

Ooh! That's what you get!

His left hand wraps into a fist around the dart.

DWAYNE

You had a dream that disclosed Tara was the
Magician, so solve the rest of the riddle, damn
it! Because the next time you fail, I'll be
choosing a more vulnerable part. Now, retrieve
those cards!

Dwayne stoops to the ground and finds four of the cards.

DWAYNE

Hey, little brother; why did you break into the
gun closet? Just who did that leave for me to
talk to? What higher cause? Shut up, Dwayne!

He locates the fifth card at the edge of the upper garden. Dwayne
gazes down at the park.

DWAYNE

Luck is in the wind, Jasmine. I just spotted her.

EXT. GOLDEN GATE PARK - DAY

June strolls up to a yoga-sitting Lola.

                    LOLA
        I like your manicure.

                    JUNE
        Thanks. No wonder this is your favorite spot --
        plenty of men.

Lola stretches.

                    LOLA
        Oh, that dog walking a stranger? Dwayne told me
        I was an empress before he asked for my phone
        number. How could I refuse?

INT. DESTINY AND MADELEINE'S HALLWAY - DAY

JAZZ plays softly. Tara: Another plain outfit, another scarf, her
antique suitcase parked nearby. Destiny's bold attire strikes a
contrast.

                    TARA
        That's such a pretty name: Destiny.

                    DESTINY
        I treated myself to it when I turned twenty.

                    TARA
        What was your name before?

                    DESTINY
        Fate.

                    TARA
        Oh yeah?

                    DESTINY
        I picked that on my eighteenth birthday.

Destiny and Tara wander into

THE KITCHEN

Where Destiny opens a closet to divulge many
liquor bottles.

DESTINY

Lots of medicine inside. Help yourself to a cure
anytime.

TARA

That won't be necessary.

DESTINY

By the way, we all share dishes, and we get upset
if you leave them overnight. We get roaches.

Tara picks up a glass on the counter.

TARA

For some pills.

The tour continues back into THE HALLWAY.

Where both stop outside a room. A "PLEASE KNOCK FIRST" sign
but Destiny just opens the door. JAZZ louder. Madeleine in
used painter's overalls while "a different beret a day" is fast
becoming her trademark.

Artistic materials for sculpture and painting including an
easel and stool. A canvas, backside out, leans against the wall.
Madeleine sculpts an elongated figure.

DESTINY

Hey, Madeleine, this is Tara. She's staying in
the "petite suite."

Madeleine stops working.

MADELEINE
(bites a nail)
Hi. Let me know if there is something you need.

Destiny shuts the door. Music QUIETER.

                    DESTINY
You met Madeleine so there is no need to disturb
her again -- she gets very busy with her art.

INT. TARA'S ROOM - DAY

The little room Tara and Destiny find themselves in contains a
bureau, a desk, a window, and a mattress on the floor with some
bedding. Suitcase grounded; Tara places her glass on the desk.

                    DESTINY
Petite... it sounds much nicer than tiny. The
landlord even promises to knock out a wall...
someday.

                    TARA
I wasn't expecting a penthouse.

                    DESTINY
Just so you don't have a fear of suffocation.

                    TARA
No more than the next person.

                    DESTINY
Hanging is supposed to bring on a great orgasm.
Of course, your neck breaks.

                    TARA
That's... morbid.

                    DESTINY
So what do you like to do?

                    TARA
Sing.

                    DESTINY
Interesting. I'm collaborating with a vocalist
myself; I might have something for you.

Destiny grasps Tara's clothed neck.

                              TARA
     Yes?

                            DESTINY
          I've always wanted a scarf like that.

Tara removes the neckwear and hands it to Destiny.

                              TARA
          It's yours. Thanks for letting me stay here.

                            DESTINY
          Don't sweat the small stuff.

Destiny leaves, closing the door. Tara opens her suitcase.

INT. DESTINY'S ROOM - DAY

Destiny retrieves a voodoo doll from a bureau drawer. Its head
features Tara's picture. She ties the scarf around the doll's
neck.

                            DESTINY
                        (to the doll)
          You enjoy jogging at the beach but can't swim.
          Then, there's your fondness for alcohol and,
          also, singing. Well, try this octave on for size.

She tightens the scarf.

INT. TARA'S ROOM - DAY

Unpacking ceases. Tara chokes, coughs, and holds her throat! The
room spins a couple times around her. Tara flops onto the bed
and breathes a sigh of relief.

INT. DESTINY'S ROOM - DAY

Destiny clutches the scarf in one hand and the doll in the other.

                            DESTINY
                        (to the doll)
          That was only a scare.

                        DESTINY
            You'll know when I break the rules.

EXT. MICHAEL'S GARDEN - DAY

Michael on a bench, open Bible on his lap -- eyes closed.

                        MICHAEL
            Holy Father, plenty of people live in tough
            environments. Besides, temptation can't happen
            if I avoid the person.

EXT. FIELD - DAY - MICHAEL'S VISION

Straw. Two religious symbols materialize in statue form: Jesus
and the Virgin Mary. The view turns to their backsides.

RETURN TO GARDEN

Concern occupies Michael's face as he opens his eyes.

INT. DION'S LIVING ROOM - DAY

Lola braids Dion's hair.

                        DION
            No one's a bystander at a group vibration. So,
            peek.

June opens the large cedar chest; it contains various small
instruments; she grabs a bongo.

                        JUNE
            I played drums in high school.

Lola strums bass guitar and sings back-up vocals. Dion croons a
few verses from "HARMONY" and plays the piano. June's drum keeps
the beat. A brass sculpture of Lord Shiva shimmers; a mandala
on a wall shows off its web.

In conclusion, all three hit and hold an "ooh" vocal. They drift
toward a standing circle.

                         DION
Two sexy women -- keep vibrating.

                         LOLA
              (starts to unzip her dress)
I've always liked... spontaneous.

                         JUNE
            (begins to unbutton her blouse)
None of this should leave the room.

                         LOLA
Trust, darling.

Their circle tightens as the undressing gets rapid!

INT. HOTEL - DAY

Holding a camera in front of himself, Michael walks along a
decorated hallway before knocking at a door. Wesley opens caring
a comic book as Michael raises the camera.

                         WESLEY
Why are you pointing that thing at me, Michael?

                         MICHAEL
Just a... question for the record. No one's
been... you know, paid.

                         WESLEY
It's an entire money process -- investors,
domestic and foreign distribution rights, deal
points. You just worry about your own little
creative juices.

                         MICHAEL
But when?

                         WESLEY
Trust me. It will happen soon. Meanwhile, keep
the big picture in mind.

31.

                    MICHAEL
Don't wait too long, Wesley. The natives are
getting restless.

                    WESLEY
              (waves the comic)
I'm taking a short break but I'm still quite
busy trying to get everyone their money. So
don't shove your little camera in my face again;
that's stupid and impolite.

Wesley slams the door as Michael leaves.

INT. TARA'S ROOM - DAY

Glass of water in hand, a wincing Tara takes a pill and puts the
glass down near two small bottles on the desk. "TAKE AS NEEDED
FOR HEADACHES" and "TAKE AS NEEDED FOR NAUSEA."

Ready for the next move, Tara's chess set also rests on the desk.
Tara shifts around as she kneads the back of her head.

                    TARA
    Not now. Go away. Oh, that hurts!

Kneading continues.

INT. DESTINY AND MADELEINE'S BATHROOM - NIGHT

Mismatched bras and panties costume both Destiny and Madeleine.
Belly button ring glistens on the former.

Steam floats over a filled tub. Madeleine and Destiny anoint the
bath with oils, herbs, orange peels, and flower petals. A large
porcelain pitcher with white liquid lies on the floor.

                    DESTINY
So you never think of hot wax while milk is
pouring?

                    MADELEINE
Of course not. It would be perverting a naturally
sensual experience.

                         DESTINY
The wax would have to be dispensed quickly.
There isn't much time before it hardens.

                        MADELEINE
You ought to be in a museum, not just work
for one.

                         DESTINY
I wonder what position I'd like to be stuck in.

Destiny strikes a couple of poses.

INT. DESTINY AND MADELEINE'S KITCHEN - NIGHT

Tara heats both a tan and a red colored tea. She places cups
and a tray of cookies on the kitchen table where her chess set
lies ready for Move 5.

INT. DESTINY AND MADELEINE'S BATHROOM - NIGHT

In the bath, Destiny and Madeleine caress each other's faces.
Nipple rings adorn Destiny's breasts. Madeleine's right breast is
home to a small rose tattoo. Ears get tongued. They pour milk
on each other from the large pitcher. Loving laughter spells joy
for Madeleine but Destiny shudders as milk showers over her.

Destiny plants a gentle kiss on her girlfriend, then stands, and
grabs a towel. Doorbell RINGS.

                         DESTINY
In my ideal world, I wouldn't mind sharing.

                        MADELEINE
That's up to Michael.

INT. DESTINY AND MADELEINE'S HALLWAY - NIGHT

A jacket clad Michael walks behind Tara who is heading for
the kitchen. Michael stops at the bathroom door. It's open; he
glances in. It is not apparent what he sees. Michael proceeds
into

33.

THE KITCHEN

Where Tara pours a cup of tea from each vessel before seating herself. Michael comes up to the table, does 5 White PxP, and removes her pawn. He remains standing. Tara plays Black Kt-QR4, then hands Michael a cup of tan colored tea.

                    TARA
          Herbs are remedies. I made chamomile to soothe
          your tensions away.

                    MICHAEL
          And your tea?

                    TARA
          Red Clover.

                    MICHAEL
          What's that for?

Tara encounters an awkward moment. Michael puts his cup down.

                    MICHAEL
          Anyway, I'm going to be with Madeleine for the
          rest of the evening.

Michael exits. In disbelief, Tara watches him leave.

She gets up, spilling her tea. Red liquid parades off the tabletop.

INT. DESTINY AND MADELEINE'S BATHROOM - NIGHT

Alone in the tub, Madeleine watches hot water steam into a fresh bath before turning off the faucet. Michael holds her different colored bra and panties.

                    MICHAEL
          I would always need them to match.

                    MADELEINE
Fascinating what you're fascinated by.

He rubs the panties between his fingers and thumb.

                    MICHAEL
          Plenty soft though.

INT. DESTINY AND MADELEINE'S KITCHEN - NIGHT

On hands and knees, Tara uses a cloth to wipe up the spilled
liquid.

                    TARA
                 (whispers)
          No more roles. Enlightenment -- right now.

Attempting to stand, Tara bangs her head on the table.

                    TARA
          Ow!

More tea spills.

                    TARA
          Shit.

Tara rises, tosses her rag at the fridge, grabs a bottle of
Scotch from the cabinet, and rushes out. Tea drips onto the floor
as a door OPENS and shuts.

                    BROTHER ROBERT (V.O.) - DAY
          You have enough challenges so why take on
          chess? It's war; it's a battle of egos and you
          could easily give in to temptation.

                    TARA (V.O.)
          I'm over that, Brother Robert.

INT. DESTINY AND MADELEINE'S BATHROOM - NIGHT

Kneeling behind the tub, Michael washes Madeleine's back. His
jacket sleeves get damp as he soaps Madeleine's breasts. She
grasps his watch.

                         MADELEINE
          Geez... it's getting wet.

                          MICHAEL
          Waterproof.

                         MADELEINE
          Good.

Madeleine presses his hand down toward her nether world. Michael's
jacket arm gets soaked. Her hand comes back above the surface
while his watch continues to test its warranty.

                         MADELEINE
                         (wiggles)
          Ooh! I'll give you ten minutes to cut that out.

EXT. SAN FRANCISCO - STREET - NIGHT

Tara swaggers forth, taking a swig as she passes a convenience
store. She stops to stare at her bottle of booze. Her words are
slurred.

                           TARA
          Too late! The tumor's got first dibs on me.
                         (takes a swig)

Like father, like daughter. I do miss... our wonderful hugs, your
wonderful stories.

She settles down at curbside.

                           TARA
          Let your cup runneth over with song. Your last
          words to me... okay...

Contents poured into gutter as she rises.

                           TARA
          I'm getting... excellent at never again.

Tara taps the bottle against a nearby parking meter.

INT. DESTINY'S ROOM - NIGHT

Destiny lies in bed staring at the "people catcher" on her nightstand. She raises the star while her fingers grasp the crystal.

                    DESTINY
          Tara, Tara.

Destiny lowers the unit back onto the nightstand; her hand moves to her side, and she shuts her eyes.

INT. TARA'S ROOM - NIGHT

Tara asleep in her bed. She gets up with a blank stare on her face. Tara sleepwalks over to the two bottles of pills on her desk.

She dumps the containers out, forms two mounds of similar looking pills, switches bottles, and sweeps the tablets into their new homes. Tara caps the containers and puts them back where they were.

EXT. DION'S PATIO - DAY

Large bushes hover against the mansion. So does a metal ladder. A garden bench gazes upon an upper deck and spa.

A stereo and a stack of towels border a sparkling pool. So does Destiny who nurses a drink while sunbathing on a chaise.

Dion, Lola, June and QUENTIN relax in elegant chairs poolside. Quentin,32, is a smartly dressed African American man. His cross earring speaks volumes.

In a pile -- some assorted color boxed floodlights, fixtures, and a long metal cylinder with a couple of holes cut in it.

Enjoying a joint, Dion eyes Quentin. He directs it Quentin's way.

                    QUENTIN
              (shakes his head)
          That junk will rot your brain.

                    DION
Free country -- you decide. Anyway, Quentin,
our group will be expressing the pulsations of
the whole earth. So, to be powerful, we need
to commit our spirits and our bodies together.
The karma is good.

Dion takes a hit.

                    LOLA
We want to use tantric energy to create a wave
of feeling that will involve everybody. It's
new... yet old.

                  QUENTIN
              (mouth twitches)
New and old? You're contradicting yourself.

                    LOLA
Okay, do you believe in the power of women?

Lola moves close to June.

                  QUENTIN
                (laughs)
Oh, they certainly have some!

Quentin glances at June's supple body.

                    LOLA
              (caresses June)
You're seeing the beautiful body, of course.
However, she is also fertility and a goddess.

                    DION
Tantrics believe in reaching the Divine
through sex.
              (smiles)

It's a wonderful religion!

Dion takes another hit.

                    QUENTIN
That's far out.

                     LOLA
Women were deified. Both the Blessed Virgin Mary
and Mary Magdalene were Divine. Thus, we weren't
always considered evil for our temptations or
relegated to being either virgins or whores.

Lola kisses June; Quentin squirms.

                     JUNE
Ooh! I'm feeling more appreciated all the time.

                     LOLA
                  (to Quentin)
There was reverence for everyone as spiritual
entities. I want my tower of lights to represent
that.

                     DION
                  (smiling)
If you don't fall off the ladder!

                    QUENTIN
This gets too far away from basic values. True
power rests with God and God alone.

                    DESTINY
Let's just try it. All we've got so far is the
ending anyway.

                    QUENTIN
Well... I won't be preaching to the choir.

Quentin hands Dion a CD. MELODY. Quentin sings "TRUE LOVE."
Destiny dances near him. During their short performance, Destiny
portrays a temptress. Quentin shrugs her off as he sings about
his wife.

At its CONCLUSION, Destiny takes a dive into the pool. June grabs
Quentin for a slow dance. Destiny shimmies out at the other end;
Lola hands her a towel.

                              LOLA
          How did Quentin have the good fortune to find
          you, anyway?

                             DESTINY
          It's the other way around. I read his newspaper
          article and found him.

                              LOLA
          Have we met before?

                             DESTINY
          Anything's possible.

INT. DION'S GUEST BEDROOM - DAY

          Solemn missionary position. Quentin goes through
          the motions with June.

                            QUENTIN
          Tell me, June!

                              JUNE
          Yes, you're giving me pleasure. Must you
          always ask?

EXT. DION'S PATIO - DAY

Destiny navigates around the perimeter of stucco walls. A latched
gate catches her attention. She unlatches it and swings the gate
open before shutting it again.

INT. MICHAEL'S LIVING ROOM - NIGHT

Tara and Michael are sitting at the chess table. Swift moves: 6
White P-Q3 Black 7 White Kt-KB3. Tara commences with Black KtxB
and removes his bishop from play. Michael conducts 8 White PxKt
and removes her knight.

Quick play: Black B-Q3 9 White Kt-B3 Black P-R3 10 White B-K3
Black P-QKt3.

                    TARA
I'm having a tough time keeping my focus.

                   MICHAEL
No excuses. It's your move.

                    TARA
How about trying something different?

                   MICHAEL
Like?

                    TARA
Strip Chess. It would be another way to keep
track of things.

                   MICHAEL
               (mulls it over)
I am a piece ahead. Will that count for something?

Tara unbuttons and takes off her blouse. Michael can't keep from
staring.

                   MICHAEL
Just rest assured. I'll keep everything on a
spiritual level.

                    TARA
I'm confident you will.

                   MICHAEL
It will be pure strip the soul. Do you study
Freud?

                    TARA
You mean that man who chain-smoked small cigars
while he talked about penis envy?

                   MICHAEL
There's a little more to it than that.

                         TARA
          I study the teachings of Jesus, Buddha, and
          Krishna.

                         MICHAEL
          Sounds like confusion and I'm confused enough
          already.

                         TARA
          No, I felt very privileged to be in the company
          of visionaries. Sometimes, I even stopped feeling
          stuck inside myself.

                         MICHAEL
          We should find some common ground and pray.

They close and open their eyes in a split-second. Michael's
staring continues.

                         MICHAEL
          You know "pray" means two opposite things
          depending how it's spelled.

                         TARA
          This bra itches.

                         MICHAEL
          I will report that; I mean, I will report our
          positions to the Chess Institute and then go
          to bed.

He hurries to the computer.

                         TARA
          What's the rush?

                         MICHAEL
          I... I'm a creature of habit -- bedtime.

Tara gets her blouse and eases over to a typing Michael.

                         TARA
          Okay then, clocaholic, one last question --

Michael rises to face Tara. She drapes the garment on his shoulder.

                    TARA
          -- does this go in your trophy case?

                    MICHAEL
          I hadn't exactly thought...

Michael runs his finger from her neckline past her bra to her exposed tummy.

                    MICHAEL
          ... place marker.

Tara grabs her coat and leaves. Michael does an arm stretch as he ambles toward his bedroom.

EXT. BLUE HERON LAKE - DAY - MICHAEL'S DREAM (FOG)

Vapor floats everywhere. Michael, flannel nightgown and sandals, scurries along a tree-lined path.

A flat raft with no one on board glides under a bridge. An array of sparks lights up the craft as it travels forth.

                    MICHAEL
          Welcome back to these shores, Madeleine. Tell
          me more about --

Madeleine pilots the boat. Wearing a full-length red gown, she is now a sultry-voiced vamp with long black hair, eye-catching make-up, and perfect nails.

                    MADELEINE
          Outermost to innermost, Michael?

The water reflects her image.

                    MADELEINE
          Petrified wood -- the knothole of time.

Michael dashes along the path.

                    MADELEINE
          Birds add brush strokes to the sky.

He veers toward the lake.

                     MICHAEL
          Deeper.

Madeleine plays with dirt at the shoreline.

                    MADELEINE
          Combination.

Kneeling on the opposite shore, Michael touches the water.

                     MICHAEL
          Setting time, setting sail.

Madeleine places a foot in the lake, then touches the pond's
wetness. She glances in Michael's direction. Lust takes over
her face. Hands on a floating clock take time backwards at high
speed.

Wind WHOOSHES. Lying sideways embraced on the raft, Michael and
Madeleine propel across the surface! Hair and robes ruffle; water
laps their bodies.

INT. MADELEINE'S BEDROOM - DAY

"People catcher" on nightstand. Madeleine, garbed for work, lifts
the starry object.

                    MADELEINE
                   (to herself)
          It's your private world, Michael. You see me
          anyway you need to.

She stores it away in its velvet pouch in a nightstand drawer.
Madeleine moves to her stool and manipulates her sculpture. Door
OPENS. Tools of the trade and a stereo on a table.

A canvas -- still backside out against the wall. Destiny provides
a neck massage.

                         DESTINY
          You could sell the sculpture for another tidy
          sum to Michael.

                         MADELEINE
          Maybe, I'll keep it.

                         DESTINY
          Of course, I'm not sure how you'll be able to
          tell when it's done.

                         MADELEINE
          The meaning comes out of hiding.

                         DESTINY
          I can relate. A quest for the elusive holy grail
          is hidden in the Tarot -- hmmmm.

                         MADELEINE
                      (bites her nails)
          What?

                         DESTINY
          That word elusive. He said it, yes.

Destiny stops the massage.

                         DESTINY
          Anyway, the medieval church didn't like personal
          quests or goddesses.

She reaches into her pocket. The High Priestess card (a crowned
holy woman sits between two pillars with a scroll on her lap and
the crescent moon at her feet) flutters onto the table.

                         DESTINY
So all but one of the major Tarot cards were driven underground
during the witch-hunts.

                         MADELEINE
          Must you carry them everywhere?

The Fool card (a well-dressed young man and his dog pause at the edge of a cliff) alights on the table.

                    DESTINY
     The only one left in our deck today is the
     Joker. It's so much more than just symbols!

Madeleine raises her arms in bewilderment.

                    MADELEINE
     In your mind! Look, assuming he is out there,
     then it's risky. You know nothing about this
     stranger.

                    DESTINY
     Ooh, I know how I can recall more about my last
     dream.

Madeleine shakes her head as she turns on the STEREO: Jazz.

                    MADELEINE
     Want some orange juice?

                    DESTINY
     No thanks.

Madeleine leaves. Destiny fiddles with the sculpture. A piece of the elongated figure breaks off; she attempts to put it back; matters get worse.

Madeleine walks through the doorway.

                    MADELEINE
     Someone should really get their own clay to
     mold. Geez!

INT. TARA'S ROOM - DAY

Tara would be a trendsetter if "bird nest" ever becomes a room style. Clothes plus the chess trophy surround the mattress on the floor. Her chess set is in the position after Black Move 10 P-QKt3.

Tara, on a mobile phone, rubs the back of her head. A glass of water and two pill bottles are nearby. She does 11 White P-KR3.

                    TARA
          Okay, I've done that. Now, put me down for a
          castle. Goodbye.

She clicks off and places the mobile on the desk before castling her black pieces.

                    TARA
          Oh, no. How did I miss that easy move?

She opens the "TAKE AS NEEDED FOR NAUSEA" bottle and reaches in for a pill.

EXT. SAN FRANCISCO - CAFE - DAY

A seated Michael holds up a small coin.

                    MICHAEL
          That's what I'm down to today, Tara -- a penny
          for your thoughts.

Tara, table-side, along with two glasses of water, and an open laptop.

                    TARA
          I'll cover coffee.

                    MICHAEL
          No tea?

                    TARA
          I do have some semblance of my own life left.

                    MICHAEL
          Don't we all?

                    TARA
          So, how about a new title, "MUTINY ON THE SET?"
          Then we could make Wesley walk the fucking
          plank! This is bullshit.

                    MICHAEL
          You've got a mouth.

The same orifice fills the frame.

                    TARA
          Very functional too.

                    MICHAEL
          If you say so.

A seated Michael gradually comes back into full view.

                    TARA
          Of course, Wesley dropped me a hint about how
          it's a career move to put my mouth somewhere
          else.

                    MICHAEL
          This rat is sleazy.

                    TARA
          I've had it with re-write this, change that;
          make the ending more powerful.

                    MICHAEL
          Wait. What you just said -- make the ending more
          powerful. It might be possible to put ourselves
          in the driver's seat if Wesley keeps taking
          advantage of everybody.

Tara touches her chin momentarily.

                    TARA
          I'm definitely in favor of that.

                    MICHAEL
          We would need to move a few things around and
          change the climax.

Tara settles all her fingers into type position.

                    TARA
Okay. Let's do some mischief!

EXT. SAN FRANCISCO - LINCOLN PARK STEPS - DAY

        Lola and Destiny climb some steps and then view
        the ocean.

INT. SAN FRANCISCO - BAR - NIGHT

        A small candelabra with two lit candles shares
        the round tabletop with two half-full exotic
        drinks. Lola and Destiny on barstools.

                    LOLA
        It was curious that you called, Destiny. You
        were in a dream I had last night and something
        I did came in very...

Lola laughs as she extends her arm.

                    LOLA
        ... handy!

                    DESTINY
        Go on!

                    LOLA
        We were climbing up this stairway.

                    DESTINY
        Any particular place?

                    LOLA
        Where San Francisco looks down at the sea --
        you wanted a view.

                    DESTINY
        Anything else.

                    LOLA
        Someone pushed me off. That's when I looked at
        my hand.

                    DESTINY
According to dream books, you were about to fly.

                    LOLA
I declare. What a great feeling! My arms felt
like wings, and I just soared!

                    DESTINY
                    (toasts)
Here's to dream travel!

Lola halts their toast in mid-air.

                    LOLA
Wait. That's it! That's why you looked familiar.
I dreamt about you once before... before we
even met. I was showing you my favorite place
in the park.

                    DESTINY
It can happen.

                    LOLA
I guess so!

They click glasses; Lola takes a gulp; Destiny follows suit.

                    LOLA
                    (glances at watch)
But, meanwhile, I can't be turning into a
pumpkin, pumpkin. Dion wants me back by twelve.

                    DESTINY
There goes your power of women philosophy.

                    LOLA
Dion only gets his power when I say yes. That's
our understanding and it works fine.

Lola plays with Destiny's hair.

                    LOLA
A peck on the cheek doesn't always do it.

                    DESTINY
          You're in luck.

They stand and make out.

                    LOLA
          Good night.

Lola exits. Destiny pulls a Tarot deck from her purse. She fans
the pack and locates The Tower card. (The Tower depicts two
people falling headfirst from a building that has been struck
by lightning).

Destiny nestles the card into the candelabra frame. Her thumbs
and forefingers extinguish both flames!

INT. TARA'S ROOM - NIGHT

Tara's unsteady gait takes her from one side of the room to the
other.

                    TARA
          Stone cold sober. So... who said it had to be a
          straight line?

She reverses direction; the zigzag continues.

                    TARA
          Beyond the ego -- no longer stuck. Enlightenment --

Tara crashes into a wall.

                    TARA
          Damn it!

EXT. DESTINY AND MADELEINE'S FRONT PORCH - DAY

On the landing: Destiny in a bright outfit with a large purse.
Tara, in a suit, comes through the open door. She sways going
down the porch steps with Destiny.

                              TARA
          The medicine in your liquor cabinet can play a
          few tricks.

                            DESTINY
          Enjoy. Hey, nice fashion sense!

                              TARA
          I would have been lost forever without your
          directions for taking the underground.

                            DESTINY
          Don't sweat the small stuff.

EXT. SAN FRANCISCO - HIDDEN GARDEN STEPS - DAY

          These panoramic artistic garden steps move along
          at a fast pace.

INT. DION'S LIVING ROOM - DAY

Dion, eyes downward, chair and cigarette bound, plays the
electric keyboards. Butts smolder.

Lola, fidgety, tugs at her hair. She wears pants plus a sheer
blouse that does zero to hide her breasts. On a side table, an
empty wine bottle and a leather bra with pointed cups look like
they belong at the same party.

                             LOLA
Di-on! I have something important to tell you. Why don't you
pay attention?

She coughs, unbuckles her belt, and drops her pants down enough
to divulge pink panties.

                             LOLA
          Ahem! Beautiful damsel in dire distress.

Lola pulls her pants up. She reaches into the side table drawer
and draws out an open box of assorted French ticklers. She flings
them one, even two at a time at Dion. He continues playing.

Lola picks up the bottle and fakes throwing it at him while she speaks.

                    LOLA
        Plenty of men would love to be in your place.
        They'd treat me like the belle of the ball.

Lola puts the bottle back on the table. She spots her bra and picks it up. Lola runs it over the keyboards and Dion's fingers before guiding the garment along his arms.

                    LOLA
        I don't know why it is that you have such a
        hold over me. I just ache for you and you don't
        give a damn.

In one motion, Dion stops playing, grabs the bra, and smacks Lola across the waist with it!

                    DION
        I never should have let you see Destiny. Now,
        can't you tell I'm working?

Dion resumes playing. Lola wanders back toward the sofa.

                    LOLA
        You can really be a friggin' son of a bitch.

                    DION
        Leave my mother out of this.

                    LOLA
        The phone call I got this morning was from
        that gracious gentleman I met in the park. He
        offered me this great paying job. So, I wanted
        to talk it over.

                    DION
        If you think you're going to distract me,
        forget it.

                    LOLA
            (increasing loudness)
You make me feel invisible. Look at me, Dion;
I'm talking to you!

Dion stops his ivory action and glares at Lola.

                    DION
No, you're not; you're screaming at me!

                    LOLA
              (still loud)
Well, I'm getting your attention.

                    DION
Sit down and shut up! We have company coming.

Lola does a prance called forlorn. Dion points at the sofa.

                    DION
Do it!

She gives in.

                    DION
No wonder I'm getting nowhere with my career.
Now, get back up and find every one of those
French ticklers!

INT. DION'S LIVING ROOM - LATER

June and Quentin nearby. Dion and Lola group together with Tara
and Destiny.

                    DION
We pursue the sacred that is beyond the surface
of things.

                    TARA
The material world may be sacred too.

Tara notices the sword in its sheath on the wall rack.

                         TARA
Is this an antique?

                         LOLA
It's an ancient heirloom that's been with Dion's
family for many generations. The sword brings
only love and peace to its owners. It works
for us!

Everyone laughs.

                         DION
It's sharp enough to do plenty of evil, too, in
the wrong hands.

                         LOLA
Meanwhile, you and your ancestors Dion have had
plenty of time to train it.
                    (to Quentin)

Right, Mr. Reporter?

                       QUENTIN
The sword has had quite a few different owners
starting from the Middle Ages. It was considered
a gateway to the Holy Grail back then.

                         LOLA
                      (smiles)
If swords could talk.

                         JUNE
And we're glad they don't.

                       QUENTIN
The jewels alone are worth --

                       DESTINY
Hey. Is Tara going to get a chance to sing?

                         DION
Sure.

Tara hands Dion a CD. MUSIC. Tara croons "MAN FROM SOMEWHERE." She takes off her jacket to perform. The verses describe a homeless man found frozen to death in a park.

Destiny wanders off, pulls the voodoo doll out of her purse, and stabs its forehead 3 times with a large pin! Tara misses 3 lyrics, then cuts her singing short. TUNE halts as she stops the CD player.

> TARA
>
> I blanked out; don't know. It was about someone close.

> DION
>
> What I heard sounded fine.

> JUNE & QUENTIN
>
> Yeah!

> LOLA
>
> The energy is there.

> JUNE
>
> We still need publicity shots.

> DESTINY
>
> How about going out on the Bay?

EXT. DION'S PATIO - DAY

The rooftop holds a long, upright cylinder with various color flood lights attached.

INT. MICHAEL'S LIVING ROOM - DAY

A RINGING phone interrupts Michael's bookworm activity.

> MICHAEL
>
> Hello.
>   (listening)

You just made a lucky guess, sir; my place is a pigsty. Wait a minute; is this some belated gift from my chess coach? He always said my house was a mess.

INT. DWAYNE'S LIVING ROOM - DAY

Body armor and military toys co-exist. Dwayne, on a cell phone, tosses darts into a perforated wood-paneled wall.

                    DWAYNE
          How do you know your name didn't just come to me
          in a dream? Look, it's a free trial offer and all
          my employees are stars. I have an appointment
          available Tuesday morning.

Jasmine saunters past a world globe on the coffee table.

                    DWAYNE
          But Dwayne is sure there are plenty of other
          people who would gladly --

INT. MICHAEL'S LIVING ROOM - DAY

                    MICHAEL
                    (nods)
          Okay, yes, it does sound like one helluva deal!
          That'll be fine.
                    (glances at watch)

I've got to go now.

INT. MADELEINE'S BEDROOM - DAY

Closet door open. Madeleine lays a dress, blouse, and shoulder length curly blond wig in the correct anatomical positions compared to panties and a padded bra, both black, on the bed.

EXT. SAN FRANCISCO - HILL - DAY

Dwayne bounds up steep stairs carrying a small case. He runs to the top landing, takes a pair of binoculars out and gazes around.

                              DWAYNE
                        (short of breath)
             How does all this add up? Just plenty of damned
             stairs again, the ocean view...

He raises the binoculars to his eyes.

                              DWAYNE
             ... some stucco houses, the skyline... I'll be
             damned! It's the tower I dreamt about last
             night. I bet I'll recognize the floor plan too!
             The gate provides easy access and... Dwayne
             doesn't need dreams anymore; blood spilling is
             real!

EXT. DION'S PATIO - NIGHT

MELODY contains both spatial and Eastern elements. Dion, Lola,
Tara, Destiny, Quentin, and June -- colored lighting effects pour
down on all of them. Vases of flowers abound.

Tara -- colorful, silk pant suit. June -- dress with fringe, low
cut, and scary short.

Only body adornments clothe the other two women. Destiny, one
breast uncovered, glistens in a soft yarn and glass bead toga.
Just one narrow strand of crystal-strewn white velvet hangs from
Lola's neck to her nether region!

Dion and Quentin wear sarongs. All six mingle in a loose circle.
Starting with Lola, each in turn sips from a pewter goblet. The
goblet reaches Tara; she sniffs the contents before passing it
back to Lola.

                              TARA
             Nice bouquet.

Lola puts the goblet down and leads as they all place their arms
around each other; the circle tightens.

                              LOLA
             Bless our unions in this sacred world -- the
             circle is cast. Please share something personal.

                            JUNE
          It's vital to trust people.

                            TARA
          Each moment is precious.

          Dion nods as he takes in her words.

                            DION
          I feel this sense of power. I want to lead and
          make our whole troupe successful.

                            LOLA
          Jealousy is garbage.

                            QUENTIN
                    (drops his arms)
          Private thoughts were meant to stay private,
          thank you.

INT. DION'S LIVING ROOM - NIGHT

New Age MUSIC with a drumbeat, occasional female laughter plus
candles, and mood lamps. Silver platters contains what's left of
finger food including arum rolls, sushi, olives, caviar, cheese,
and crackers.

Several empty bottles of wine surround goblets. June finishes
her drink. Dion smokes weed; June takes a hit.

Tara and Quentin: Wallflowers. Lola, cherry between her lips.
June accepts her offer. Smooch.

Dwayne peers in from outside the sliding glass door before
disappearing from view.

June drops a plump strawberry down her costume; Lola undoes the
strap of June's attire while Dion recovers the fruit. June's only
garment falls away; she lies prone on the floor!

                            JUNE
          Decorate me.

Lola sprays whipped cream on June's breasts and thighs; Dion adds strawberries. June pulls Dion toward her. Lips lock. Quentin, framed against the sword rack, crosses himself. Tara remains stoic.

INT. DION'S LIVING ROOM - LATER

Whipped cream covers Destiny's exposed breast plus both of Lola's. The ladies are busy finger-painting each other. Dion relaxes on the sofa.

> DION
> (waves Quentin over)
> Quentin, come join us. It's all pure sensuality
> right now.

On a far chair, Quentin, mouth twitching, holds up his hands in self-defense. Quentin followed by Tara exit through the sliding patio door. The latter closes it shut.

Destiny and Lola stand next to a candelabrum with three burning candles.

> DESTINY
> Let's shower together, then spa.

Dion stops by.

> LOLA
> How about sharing something about yourself
> first?

Destiny extinguishes all three lit candles with her mouth!

> DESTINY
> (smiles)
> Wimps!

> DION
> Yeah!

DISSOLVE TO:

INT. DION'S LIVING ROOM - NIGHT

The rack is missing its sword and sheath.

EXT. DION'S PATIO - NIGHT

A spa holding four occupants churns. Quentin and Tara occupy a garden bench.

                    QUENTIN
     I don't find anything about this night sacred;
     totally sinful is more like it!

                    TARA
     Sensitivity does seem to be missing.

                    QUENTIN
     Take away the god and goddess outfits that Lola
     provided and you're left with only one thing: a
     swinger's club.

                    TARA
     If I may be so bold then, why are you even here?

                    QUENTIN
     We started as Dion and Lola's friends. Then I
     decided to do an article on their sword. Plus,
     I liked having the chance to sing.

                    QUENTIN
                    (pauses)
     There was one personal thing I could have
     shared but never in front of a bunch of people.

                    TARA
     I'm listening.

                    QUENTIN
                    (mouth twitches)
     June, she... I want to satisfy her but it's
     like... never happening.

                    TARA
     I'm sure you're happy together in other ways.

                              QUENTIN
          I... I've got to get out of this ridiculous
          costume!

Quentin rambles toward the house.

EXT. DION'S UPPER DECK - SPA - NIGHT

Dion, Lola, June, and Destiny lounge in the spa. The jets muffle
their small talk. Towels and robes await their duty. Tara remains
on the garden bench, her eyes closed, and hands in prayer
position below her lips.

Dwayne emerges from bushes near the patio door and darts along
a shadowy walkway. The sword in its sheath -- discernible for
an instant before he transfers it to the front of his body. Just
prior to the ajar gate, Dwayne trips and falls to the ground;
metal hits concrete! The sound startles Tara awake.

                              TARA
          What's going on there!?

Dwayne, along with his stolen goods, manages to escape the patio.

EXT. DION'S ESTATE GROUNDS - NIGHT

Tara runs helter-skelter chasing a silhouette who flees among
the trees.

                              DWAYNE
          I can't slay you yet! You don't have it.

Tara loses ground; the subject of her pursuit vanishes.

EXT. DION'S PATIO - NIGHT

Destiny, dressed in a towel, stands at the gate. Tara re-enters
holding one hand to her head briefly.

                              TARA
          I've never felt so dizzy.

                              DESTINY
          What happened?

Destiny takes Tara's arm; they move toward the pool.

                                TARA
          Someone was up to no good... probably stealing
          something.

                              DESTINY
          The shadows can play tricks this time of night.

                                TARA
          I haven't seen too many shadows trip over
          themselves or talk.

                              DESTINY
          Talk?

                                TARA
          Just a death threat.

Wrapped in spa robes, Dion, Lola, and June approach.

                              DESTINY
          She thinks she saw Robin Hood.
                         (to Tara)

You need this.

Destiny places her arms around Tara and glides with her into
the pool. Destiny, separated from her towel, swims away. Tara
encounters difficulty staying afloat, then sinks!

June spots the trouble, sheds her robe, and dives in. She
resurfaces holding Tara who coughs out water.

                                TARA
                       (gasping for breath)
          Thanks! I never learned to swim.

Destiny slithers out at the opposite side.

DESTINY
(to herself)
I'll make a note.

INT. MADELEINE'S BEDROOM - NIGHT

A cross dressed but shoeless Michael sits on the side of Madeleine's bed. He wears the outfit Madeleine had set out, including the curly blond wig.

MADELEINE
Geez, don't we look pretty?

MICHAEL
I'm expecting women's intuition to kick in at any time.

Madeleine carries a pair of high heel shoes.

MADELEINE
Here's the reason for this whole charade. Admit it!

She fits them on Michael.

MICHAEL
Platform wedges. You're really broadening my horizons.

She touches her tongue and flicks one finger as she bites a nail.

MADELEINE
There's a lot to broaden. Now, show off the whole ensemble for me.

Michael treads around the room.

MADELEINE
The feeling?

MICHAEL
Bondage and power at the same time.

                    MADELEINE
          You always wanted to be the chess queen.

Michael spots himself in the mirror.

                    MICHAEL
          I, uh, trust this'll stay our little secret.

She taps her nightstand.

                    MADELEINE
          Yep. It'll go in my secret drawer.

                    MICHAEL
          See, I'm not so strait-laced as you thought,
          Madeleine.

                    MADELEINE
          Touche. Your point.

                    MICHAEL
          So... want to undress a woman and make love to
          a man?

                    MADELEINE
          I've never been propositioned like that before!

Amidst their giggles, the base of the tall figure sculpture
receives some clothes. The artwork is between them as they catch
their breath.

                    MADELEINE
          The sculpture is for you -- my gift.

                    MICHAEL
          But you need the money.

                    MADELEINE
          From benefactor to boyfriend.

                    MICHAEL
                    (smiles)
          I'm just glad your kissing offer is still --

Madeleine kisses Michael in an embrace that takes them bedside; more clothes come off in the height of passion.

EXT. SAN FRANCISCO - MAIDEN LANE - OUTDOOR CAFE - DAY

Birds fly down the alley toward Union Square.

Madeleine is parked at the table along with two coffees and a folder. However, she is missing her beret.

> MADELEINE
> Nothing would be more stupid than people getting caught by their own video.

Michael table-side.

> MICHAEL
> Or more challenging either, Madeleine. Besides, we're going to stay one step ahead of any problems.

> MADELEINE
> (smiles)
> Let's make that two or three steps.

> MICHAEL
> Michael's left hand pushes a folder to Madeleine. She finds some papers inside and shuffles through them.

> MADELEINE
> Just right for my "landscape period." Looks like more artwork for me to do.

> MICHAEL
> Make this your "realism period." Meanwhile, the whole plan stops in a heartbeat if everyone gets their money.

Madeleine places the documents back in the folder.

                    MADELEINE
Anyway, you can probably guess what Wesley
wanted me to do to, pardon the pun, get ahead
in my career.

                    MICHAEL
No guesses -- just one last thing. Buy the most
expensive fuel -- no messy buildup, no residue.

                    MADELEINE
We just might get away with this.
                    (winks)

You do sweat the small stuff!

Two coffee mugs click in mid-air as arms intertwine.

EXT. MICHAEL'S GARDEN - NIGHT

In rapid succession: 12 White P-R3 Black Q-K2 13 White Q-Q2 Black
B-KB4 14 White Q-K2 Black B-R2 15 White P-KKt4 Black Kt-K5 16
White KtxKt Black BxKt.

A blouse, a man's shirt, a winged tip shoe, and a high heel
shoe inhabit a bench. Otherwise fully dressed, Michael and Tara
continue their chess contest while seated.

White Move 17 R-KKt1. Tara kicks off her remaining high heel
shoe. Black Q-B3

                    MICHAEL
I'm curious about the cloistered life.

                    TARA
The Zen Monastery was a great escape. But, after
a while, I was just trading one set of rules
for another.

                    MICHAEL
Rules can be good.

                    TARA
So you could be celibate and survive?

Michael stands and paces a bit.

                    MICHAEL
        Celibacy -- can that be started with a cold
        shower?

                    TARA
                    (smiles)
        You're always searching. What was growing up
        like?

                    MICHAEL
        The truth?

                    TARA
        There's a thought.

                    MICHAEL
        Lonely.

                    TARA
        It shows.

                    MICHAEL
        What do you mean?

                    TARA
        Sometimes, when I see you and you think no one
        is looking; well, you have this expression when
        you let your guard down --

                    MICHAEL
        That's enough.

                    TARA
        What are you afraid of?

He drops into a chair.

                    MICHAEL
        I've never said I love you to anyone.

TARA

Not even to your parents?

MICHAEL

It was... awkward. And a grandmaster doesn't always make a master parent.

TARA

I was sixteen when my father took off for the last time. He was eventually found homeless and dead. We never even said goodbye; who knew?

MICHAEL

I find comfort in games.

TARA

It's not exactly a hidden obsession. Become the results and it's possible to win even when you lose.

MICHAEL

What? Did somebody write a book about the power of negative thinking?

TARA

No. Just something to chew on.

MICHAEL

Well, sink your teeth into this.

He proceeds with 18 White R-Kt3. Tara removes her brassiere.

TARA

Had your rabies shots?

Tara plays Black BxKt and trots the knighted horse off the board. Michael takes off his remaining shoe.

Fast Pace: 19 White RxB Black Q-R5 20 White R-Kt3 Black P-K5 21 White R-KKt1 Black QxRP 22 White Castles Black Q-B6 23 White Q-Q2 Black P-QR4 24 White K-Kt1 Black P-KB3 25 White R-R1 Black K-B2 26 White QR-Kt1 Black K-K2 27 White Q-K1 Black B-B5 28 White R-R4 Black R-KKt1 29 White QR-R1 Black P-KKt4 30 White RxP.

DISSOLVE TO:

EXT. SAN FRANCISCO BAY - SAILBOAT - DAY

Waves lap around the side of a large yacht. A CREW of two handle the sailing. Dion, Lola, Quentin, June, Tara, and Destiny are on board.

In a sketchbook, Lola draws in details of a large, pillared stage. The city skyline looks like a postcard behind her. Dion sits between Lola and his boom box. He finishes a cigarette.

> DION
>
> The theft of my sacred saber is nothing less than disastrous. One ripple affects the whole pond.

> LOLA
>
> If it was meant to be, your sword will find its way home.

Lola rubs her foot against Dion's ankle causing a slight smile on the recipient. With a small camera in neck strap position, Destiny moves close to the boat's edge; Tara is alongside.

> DESTINY
>
> So stop chasing snakes. They can turn around and bite you.

> TARA
>
> But I feel guilty. There was a time when I could have caught up with that thief.

> DESTINY
>
> Guilt doesn't do anyone any good. Things get stolen. It happens.

> TARA
>
> The dark side does like to swallow up the light.

> DESTINY
>
> Sure, it's called nighttime. The world is built on opposites.

Destiny whips out and brushes the Devil Tarot card (a winged Satan sits on a small box while a nude man and woman stand chained to the cubicle) across Tara's face. Tara steps back.

                         TARA
          What was that for?

                         DESTINY
          Sometimes, evil seeks fun for its own sake. You
          can practically count on it.

Destiny tucks the card away. Tara moves toward Destiny.

                         TARA
          I remain Dion's best hope for getting his sword
          back. That's what you can count on.

Destiny directs Tara into some modeling poses at the edge of the boat. Tara is a willing subject for pictures but keeps her outfit on. Destiny moves in for a body touching close-up.

                         TARA
          Enough!

Tara bumps back into Destiny.

Dion powers up the BOOM BOX; it plays cuts from Dion, Quentin, and Tara's repertoire during the photo shoot. Dion and Destiny take turns with the camera. Some of the shots appear as instant still photos. A lackluster Quentin remains fully dressed for pictures, but June gets topless.

Destiny is down to a thong. Lola makes a sport out of flashing for pictures. Dion, in a speedo, shows off his physique. Lola pours wine into glasses for June, Dion, and Destiny. Tara grabs a mineral water.

                         LOLA
                       (toasts)
          May our circle remain unbroken and guide us
          through even the roughest waters!

June lifts her glass and holds it out to sea.

                              JUNE
            Our first gig will be happening before we know
            it. Bottoms up!

Everybody except Quentin toasts that statement. June downs the
wine and refills. Dion, very much into it now, turns the volume
up full blast.

INT. MICHAEL'S LIVING ROOM - DAY

Madeleine's figure sculpture looks on as Michael, in his club
chair, thumbs to a spot in the dictionary.

                            MICHAEL
            "Trifolium Pratense -- A clover that has red
            flowers and is grown for forage."

He rises and places the book atop one of several stacks of
hardbacks that are competing for attention on the floor.

                            MICHAEL
            Just check with an authority.

Michael ambles over to the phone and picks up the receiver.

EXT. SAN FRANCISCO BAY - SAILBOAT - DAY

Quentin and a dressed June, seated together. June, inebriated,
holds forth with a glass of Chardonnay. Quentin clutches a
crossword puzzle magazine.

                            JUNE
            This is quite a nice boat.

                            QUENTIN
            It's just overcrowded.

                            JUNE
            What do you mean by that?

                            QUENTIN
            I'm not in the mood to discuss it.

                         JUNE
Well, I am in the mood. This whole group thing
is based on openness. So why hide anything?

                        QUENTIN
As if you care. I was a total loner the other
night: the more into it you got, the more out
of it I felt!

                         JUNE
There's no reason for that; you know how much
I love you.

                        QUENTIN
Dion sees this whole thing as one big free-for-all.

                         JUNE
Maybe, you're envious because he is open to
many things.

                        QUENTIN
You're missing the whole point! No wonder you
think that some other man touching your body
is fine.

                         JUNE
Look, Dion, silver spoon and all, did recover
after being burned in business by his best
friend. He says lovemaking is the cure.

                        QUENTIN
How did you know that?

                         JUNE
Lola told me. So, what about Lola and me?

                        QUENTIN
That's wrong too. You're digging a hole!

He opens the magazine.

                         QUENTIN
          Help me on this. What is another word for
          infidelity?

                          JUNE
          Let me explain... truth. This was only meant to
          loosen everyone up so we could get to know each
          other. It was supposed to be just fun and games.

                         QUENTIN
          Is that what it's come to?

Quentin turns and faces out to sea. June puts her arms around
him and presses her head flat against his back.

                          JUNE
          Quentin, don't get that way. Keep talking to
          me... don't get...

June's head shakes against her husband's back. The boat sails on.

                      LOLA AND TARA
          ~let their feet dip into the ocean.

                          LOLA
          The water is so bright and sparkling.

                          TARA
          But underneath, nature's dark womb. Oh, no...

Tara holds her mouth before throwing up overboard.

EXT. SAN FRANCISCO BAY - DOCK - DAY

Everyone comes ashore from the sailboat. SPACEY tune plays from
the boom box that rides on Dion's shoulder. Quentin carries a
satchel.

                          DION
          Music is such a great connector.

                         QUENTIN
          Trouble is you're connecting with lots of other
          things too. This free love and psychedelic stuff
          ended with the hippie era.

Dion and Quentin take a few more steps together.

                         DION
          Maybe you prefer silence, Quentin.

Dion throws the boom box to the ground; music STOPS!

                         QUENTIN
          We never even discussed music, or you'd know
          I play guitar. There's certainly communication
          around here -- static!

                         DION
          First things first. Let me thank you for
          announcing my sword to the world! So, you're
          the reporter; dig into it, get it back!

                         QUENTIN
          I've dug up something all right. It didn't come
          into your ancestors' hands in any decent way;
          they stole it. So now, it's stolen from you.
          There you go, hippie man -- karmic retribution!

Dion stares down at the boom box. His foot launches the music
machine on a short flight followed by a crash landing!

                         DION
          Bad vibrations!

EXT. SAN FRANCISCO ZOO - MERRY-GO-ROUND - DAY

The carousel revolves to music. Madeleine rides on a moving horse
while Michael's mount is a stationary animal.

                         MADELEINE
          Um... feel that breeze! Can I ask you something?
          What was it that made you want to buy my
          paintings?

                    MICHAEL
I don't know... I usually go for things that have
precise form and shape.

                    MADELEINE
To match your precise personality.

Madeleine bites a nail and flicks it out.

                    MICHAEL
Stop that. It's... irritating. Okay, I'm not so
spontaneous.

                    MADELEINE
That's the understatement of a lifetime.

                    MICHAEL
What is this, Criticize Michael Day?

                    MADELEINE
Well, Creature of Habit! Who else always buttons
his shirt all the way to the top... unless, of
course, he's wearing a blouse!

                    MICHAEL
Are you going to keep bringing up that experiment
from the other night, Madeleine? It was one time
only.

Michael fastens his top button.

                    MICHAEL
I got in the habit, so I have a place to tuck
in my dinner napkin.

                    MADELEINE
Oh, gawd...

                    MICHAEL
Listen, Ms. Free Spirit. Just because I try to
have some solid habits and one relationship at
a time in my life...

                         MADELEINE
What life? Your life is in all these books!

                          MICHAEL
Well, at least I read instead of sleeping with
whoever happens to catch my fancy.

                         MADELEINE
Well, maybe you should try it sometime! I can't
get everything I want from just one person.

                          MICHAEL
Who says?

                         MADELEINE
Just wake up! This is life, not fiction!

                          MICHAEL
You know, I thought we had a lot more in common.

                         MADELEINE
Another thing --

                          MICHAEL
I'm getting dizzy...
                      (dismounts)

... it's time to get off this ride... for good!

Michael exits the merry-go-round.

                         MADELEINE
                  (shouting after him)
      Don't be ridiculous... it can't... Michael!

A myriad of animals twirl by on the merry-go-round. Madeleine
remains on her moving horse. Tears flow: she bites her nails.

                         MADELEINE
                       (mumbling)
You just left your perfect dream lover... I'll
never tell -- some piece of perfect I am. Geez!

INT. MICHAEL'S DINING ROOM - DAY

The two identical wall clocks, stopped at slightly different times, lie on the dining room table. Michael, wearing a jeweler's eyepiece, is doing surgery on a component. His hands shake.

                    MICHAEL
          It's so irritating, so damn irritating!

INT. DION'S ENTRYWAY - NIGHT

A caftan-clad Dion with Tara alongside. He points to the living room.

                    DION
          Make yourself comfortable. I have things to tie
          up. Then we can develop some songs.

He makes a drinking gesture with his hand.

                    DION
          What sort of firewater will it be while you're
          waiting? It's in appreciation of your fine effort
          the other night.

                    TARA
                  (smiles)
          Tap.

Tara winds her way into the

LIVING ROOM

And toward the sofa.

                    DION
          Yeah, looks like you've got a nice buzz going
          already.

INT. DION AND LOLA'S BEDROOM - NIGHT

Lola stands wearing a blouse and shorts. Leather restraints that drape over a brass canopy rail bind her wrists. Her ankles are shackled by similar cuffs. Dion grabs a leather paddle from the dresser.

                    DION
          "Tara" is your new safe word.

Dion tantalizes Lola with some taps directed against her bottom.

                    LOLA
          Ooh, that tickles. Please!

Dion pulls her shorts down and studies her bare butt. Her fingers squeeze the metal frame. Dion applies the paddle!

                    LOLA
          Yes! Ooh!

Dion turns up the heat with additional strokes.

                    LOLA
          My! Ooh!

INT. DION'S LIVING ROOM - NIGHT

Occasional MUFFLED paddling. Dion's keyboards in front of his chair. Tara on the couch, glass of water on the side table. She discovers a French tickler tucked into a cushion and examines it briefly.

                    LOLA (O.S.)
                  (from a distance)
          Ooh! Ow!

Tara pulls a mobile out of her pocket as she takes an unsteady walk toward the staircase.

                    LOLA (O.S.)
          Tara!

PADDLING stops. Tara glances upstairs before making a call. Lola appears on the landing, one leather restraint attached to her ankle and another dangling from her wrist. The blouse and shorts are intact.

LOLA
Don't be afraid. It will all be clear.

TARA
(into the phone)
Bishop takes bishop!

She clicks off and pockets the phone.

LOLA
Come upstairs.

TARA
I, uh...

LOLA
Trust me.

Tara weaves up the steps to join Lola on

THE LANDING.

Dion reigns over the top of the stairs.

DION
What was hidden remained mysterious and jewel-
like as her soul and body climbed ever upward.

LOLA
Well, I declare... you put Dion in a lyrical
mood, Tara dear.

DION
Now, proceed to my chambers for an ensemble
meeting.

Lola glances up at him.

LOLA
Can ice cream be included?

DION
You know how to ask for it better than that.

Dropping to one knee, Lola gazes up from the landing.

                    LOLA
        I scr... ea... m for ice cream.

Dion heads downstairs.

                    DION
        Women!

INT. DION AND LOLA'S BEDROOM - NIGHT

Lola closes the double doors.

                    LOLA
              (toys with Tara's hair)
        You can do anything you want with me, darling.

                    TARA
        But I never... will it mean something?

Lola places her hands, arms outstretched, on Tara's shoulders.

                    LOLA
        You're hot for me, aren't you?

Tara touches Lola's dangling wrist cuff.

                    LOLA
        I love it when I don't have a choice.

Tara locks the door.

INT. DION'S UPSTAIRS HALLWAY - NIGHT

A now naked Dion carries the ice cream in two large bowls, one
in each hand, up the stairs. He pauses outside the doors to the
master bedroom.

                    DION
        Open wide! The ice cream man is here.

Dion bangs on a door with his foot. He places the ice cream on
the floor and tries the doorknob. Locked.

                              DION
          Okay, funny joke. Now, let me in. You don't want
          to get me mad!

He shakes and jars the doors. As Dion gets set for a full-body
ram, Tara opens them.

                              TARA
          Why don't you show us some real power? Make
          your music penetrate our flesh!

She shuts the doors to

THE BEDROOM

And turns to face Lola.

                              TARA
          You two have a little trouble sharing everything
          in that circle.

                              LOLA
          You impress me....

Tara kisses Lola.

                              LOLA
          ... ooh, impress me more.

Eerie TUNE commences.

                              TARA
                    (amidst warm kisses)
          But you aren't like... out to sleep with everyone?

                              LOLA
          One tries.

Tara breaks free.

                              TARA
          I need some night air.

                              LOLA
          Please.

                              TARA
          Begging doesn't always become you.

Two bowls of slightly melted ice cream rest in front of the doors
that Tara opens. EERIE melody louder. She exits.

EXT. SAN FRANCISCO - LAND'S END BEACH - DAY

The Golden Gate Bridge provides a majestic beach backdrop. A
picnic basket and two beach bags reside on a blanket. So do
Michael, Tara, and her chess set. They have pants on with feet
bare, but Tara is topless while Michael retains his t-shirt. He
plays 31 White PxB and removes her bishop.

                              TARA
              I can change a bad mood instantly by running
              on the beach.

INT. MADELEINE'S BEDROOM - DAY

Jazz ongoing from the STEREO. Destiny lies nude on the bed, her
feet resting on a window ledge.

Madeleine commences painting the vagina on the canvas now
facing forward on the easel. It's a nude of Destiny merging with
colorful shapes.

                          MADELEINE
              I'll figure out someday why I saved this part
              for last. Can you think of a reason?

                           DESTINY
              I'm thinking I directed Robin Hood to a
              treasure only to lose contact. Must be too much
              interference from that "petite suite" down the
              hall!

                          MADELEINE
          I'd say your reality check got lost in the mail.

                         DESTINY
          Hmmm... I wonder if people who die in their
          sleep have a death dream first.

                         MADELEINE
          If you're suggesting something illegal...

                         DESTINY
          Nah. It won't cause Tara any more harm than a
          good scare. Anyway, what could they charge me
          with, reckless dreaming?

INT. DWAYNE'S LIVING ROOM - DAY

Spinning world globe. A jewel-laden sword in its sheath leans
against the body armor. Dwayne places the Empress, the Star,
the Ace of Swords, the Magician, and the Ace of Cups down one
at a time next to each other on a side table as he figures out
the riddle.

                         DWAYNE
          That's it: The Empress turns into a Star by
          disrobing! Then my Ace of Swords forces the
          Little Magician to reveal the Holy Grail. Riddle
          solved. The precious cup will be mine...

Dwayne grabs the sword and stabs it into a blue section of the
globe on the coffee table!

                         DWAYNE
          ...Tomorrow! Whoo!

EXT. SAN FRANCISCO - LAND'S END BEACH - DAY

Picnic continues. Michael takes quick bites of his sandwich while
Tara savors each mouthful. Fast pace moves: Black QR-KB1 32 White
R-B1 Black QxKtP. Michael removes his t-shirt.

                         MICHAEL
                    (pinches his neck)
          Now, where will I put my dinner napkin?

TARA
(laughs)
Charmer!

Rapid play: 33 White Q-B3 Black K-Q2 34 White QRxP Black RxR 35 White QxR. Michael places the captured rook down and rains sand upon it.

MICHAEL
A queen can make a wreck of a castle.

Tara picks up the captured white castle, closes her fist, and dips her hand down. Her free hand glides across her fist. She turns the castle hand over to reveal that it is gone.

MICHAEL
Nice trick but stalling. It's your turn.

TARA
You needed the rest.

MICHAEL
Try me.

Play continues in rapid succession: Black K-B1 36 White R-R7 Black K-Kt1 37 White Q-B6 Black R-QB1 38 White R-Q7 Black Q-Kt8ch.

TARA
Check.

Michael makes 39 White K-R2; Tara Black QxP. Michael takes his pants off. A bathing suit is all that separates him from his birthday suit.

TARA
You can't stand losing, can you?

Michael leans down and goes with 40 White P-Q6.

MICHAEL
If you do win, there is one foolish move you
should reconsider -- giving all that prize money
to charity.

85.

                           TARA
                    (shakes her head)
         It's my best chance to help those less fortunate.

Quick moves: Black Q-B4 41 White QxKP Black K-R2 42 White P-B3
Black P-R5 43 White Q-Q5. The Golden Gate Bridge becomes scenery
again.

EXT. SHORELINE - DAY

Michael and Tara walk toward each other from opposite directions
along the beach. Tara carries a camera. Their paths begin to
cross.

                           TARA
         Has your searching ever lead to anything
         far-reaching?

                         MICHAEL
         I would hope -- closer to the Kingdom of God.
         Pursuing Eastern philosophy that's not supposed
         to need pursuit is frustrating. But with all
         that tranquility you just left...

                           TARA
         Sometimes, a first look changes everything.
         Anyway, I created a silly recipe for enlightenment
         while I was at the monastery.

                         MICHAEL
         Too much spare time, no doubt.

                           TARA
         Empathy to the nth degree with equal parts
         bliss and immortality.

                         MICHAEL
         Maybe, what's on the other side of the river
         isn't worth the swim.

                           TARA
         It's worth it. Prejudice and killing would become
         literally self-defeating.

                         MICHAEL
          Perhaps, the dead continue to live as dreamy
          other animals.

Tara touches his shoulder.

                          TARA
          That's a wild one, Michael!

He cups her breasts.

They kiss and fall all over each other onto the sand! Waves
cascade. Later, a clothed Michael fidgets on the passenger side
of a parked car. Tara brushes sand off her face.

                          TARA
             Uh, oh. Make-up -- 911.

                         MICHAEL
          Believe it or not, Wesley's company is not even
          showing up on Google!

                          TARA
          Meanwhile, you believe that video builds trust.
          So, why don't I pose the big question to you?

Michael comes back into view. Tara points her camera at him.

                         MICHAEL
          I'd like the benefit of your opinion first.

                          TARA
Yes, I would like to stay one step ahead of the bullshit. Now,
monsieur, are you greenlighting this project?

                         MICHAEL
          I should tell you my motto: Where there's smoke,
          there's fire.

                          TARA
          Feels so crazy.

                              MICHAEL
          Like two loons -- but we should give the rat
          one last chance.

Michael's face quickly fills the screen before a wild dissolve
occurs.

                              TARA
          Whoops. I pushed the wrong button. Kiss me
          anyway.

INT. TARA'S ROOM - NIGHT

A pajama-clad Tara lies prone in bed surrounded by her possessions.
She closes her eyes.

INT. ~BART SUBWAY - DAY - TARA'S DREAM

VOICE OVER ongoing. Tara takes the escalator partway down twice.
In another loop, an underground train arrives twice as Tara
waits.

                           TARA (V.O.)
          I need more time, father. I want to make you
          proud.

                          FATHER (V.O.)
          The birds think... Can you hear me?... The birds
          think they're still in paradise.

                           TARA (V.O.)
          Stay beside me.

INT. DESTINY'S ROOM - NIGHT

Destiny lies in bed holding her "people catcher." Her fingers
grasp the crystal.

                             DESTINY
          Tara, Tara.

She tosses the device toward the bottom of the bed. Her eyes
shut.

INT. ~BART SUBWAY - DAY - TARA'S DREAM

SILENCE. A "THIRD RAIL CAUTION" sign looms above the tracks.
Tara waits alone. A BART train exits the tunnel, comes to a stop,
and opens its doors. As Tara enters, Destiny's sudden appearance,
complete with metal pipe, breaks the quiet.

She pulls Tara onto the platform and slams her on the back of
the head with the pipe! Tara slumps to the ground. The station's
lights flicker as a BART train arrives and leaves. Empty tracks
again.

INT. MICHAEL'S LIVING ROOM - NIGHT - TARA'S DREAM

Madeleine's black and white abstract painting. It transitions
into a sculpture of Buddha. Then, the sculpture morphs into a
painting of Jesus.

INT. CHURCH - NIGHT - TARA'S DREAM

Organ PLAYS. Panorama of stained glass. Brother Robert has
adopted a reverend look: shirt, tie, and a black pulpit robe
emblazoned with two red crosses at chest height. Reverend Robert
stands behind the pulpit; he gestures and lectures, but his WORDS
cannot be heard.

Clad only in dark pants, Tara lies motionless in a coffin. The
medieval black chess pieces rest nearby on an altar table.

Destiny, wearing a nightgown, is all pleasure as she picks up
a castle. She holds the piece as it changes into a lit white
candle.

The lit candle becomes a nozzle attached to a rubber hose.

                         DESTINY
           Don't worry, Tara. If you have any friends,
           you'll live again... in their dreams!

Destiny sprays wax from the hose into the coffin where it lands
on Tara's feet. Next, she directs the paraffin spray toward her
victim's mid-section.

>   DESTINY
>   (giggles)
>   Morbid. Ooh, I like that name! Morbid.

Courtesy of Destiny, the hot ooze reaches Tara's exposed chest.

INT. MADELEINE'S BEDROOM - NIGHT

Resting in bed, Madeleine stares at the "people catcher" on her nightstand. Her fingers grasp its inner sanctum.

>   MADELEINE
>   Tara, Tara.

Her hand pulls back as her eyes close.

INT. CHURCH - DAY - TARA'S DREAM

Wax shrouds Tara up to her neck. An array of sparks showers the entryway at the back of the pews. They dissipate to reveal Madeleine, dressed in baby doll pajamas. She stands glaring at Destiny who lurks near the coffin.

>   DESTINY
>   (faces Madeleine)
>   Get out of here! Finders' keepers!

>   MADELEINE
>   We'll see about that!

Madeleine vanishes amidst another sea of sparks.

INT. MADELEINE'S BEDROOM - NIGHT

Madeleine, in regular pajamas, powers up her stereo: JAZZ.

INT. CHURCH - DAY - TARA'S DREAM

The jazz INCREASES in volume as the organ music DECREASES until it is silent. Many chess pieces are now lit candles. Oozing hose in hand, Destiny peers into the coffin.

Tara explodes out of the wax body cast and punches Destiny in the face! The blow sends Destiny dazed and reeling against a pillar.

                    DESTINY
          Too late. The die is cast; tomorrow comes!

Tara levels her with a second punch! Lit candles and hot wax from the flowing hose sizzle around Destiny. Reverend Robert's gestures become flamboyant while his sermon offers up perhaps his best UNHEARD words yet.

INT. TARA'S ROOM - DAYBREAK

The JAZZ hits even louder decibels around Tara, asleep on her back in bed. She darts up to the sitting position.

Tara grabs her father's trophy off the floor and clasps it to her pajama-covered body. MUSIC stops.

                    TARA
          Stay by my side, father!
                    (looks around)

Madeleine's music. There should always be time for...

Cup in hand, she makes a jagged exit.

INT. MADELEINE'S BEDROOM - DAYBREAK

Madeleine, still in her regular pajamas, is next to the easel when Tara, carrying the cup, crashes into the room!

                    TARA
          ... a hug!

After a moment of staring, they rush to an embrace!

INT. MICHAEL'S BEDROOM - DAY

Michael's bedroom door is open. The furniture is traditional with a small safe residing next to the chest of drawers. Madeleine's painting with blended smokestacks and trees hangs on the wall.

91.

Michael, in a blue bathrobe, studies his watch before looking at "FREE YOUR MIND."

                    MICHAEL
                 (reads aloud)
        "I can't touch other than my infinite Self."
                 (lowers the book)

This stuff makes less sense every time I --

Doorbell RINGS.

                    MICHAEL
                   (yells)
        Come in! The door's unlocked! I'll be right
        with you!

Door OPENS and closes.

EXT. SAN FRANCISCO - 48TH AVENUE - DAY

Dwayne marches down the street using his right hand to grip a long object tucked inside his overcoat. He disappears into the beach tunnel.

INT. MICHAEL'S FOYER - DAY

Lola removes her blouse, leaving her breasts free of clothing.

                    MICHAEL (O.S.)
        You're out of luck if you didn't bring your own
        cleaning supplies. And you might as well know
        that I've tried several housekeeper services
        and was never satisfied with any of them.

Still robed and holding his book, Michael enters. Lola, feather duster and cleaning supplies nearby, grabs his attention.

                    MICHAEL
        Housekeeping has... definitely changed! I'm
        Michael.

                         LOLA
          I'm Lola and all your books need to be put
          neatly away.

Lola takes some hardbacks from the floor to the shelf. Getting
the cue, Michael extends his arm, book in hand.

                         LOLA
          This is my first day on the job and I want to
          make sure everything is perfect.

Lola accepts the offering and places it on a nearby shelf.

                        MICHAEL
          Right, organizing would be good for me too. I
          think I'll collect my... thoughts.

He plops into a club chair.

                         LOLA
          I declare I think you're blushing, darling.

Lola travels into THE KITCHEN which is a mess. She surveys the
surroundings while playing with her hair.

                         LOLA
                     (raised voice)
          I may have to do more than just roll up my
          sleeves in here! Of course, that's only a phrase
          at this point.

                      MICHAEL (O.S.)
          Fine with me! Whatever it takes to get everything
          clean.

Lola undresses down to her panties. Michael enters.

                        MICHAEL
          What the...?

                         LOLA
          Am I doing something wrong?

                    MICHAEL
No, not at all. You're doing great! However, I'm
going to find out in a second that I'm still
dreaming.

                    LOLA
I'll take that as a compliment.

                    MICHAEL
Mind if I watch... you clean? You seem so...
sweet.

                    LOLA
Of course, you're supposed to watch! That's the
purpose of hiring an exotic maid.

                    MICHAEL
The purpose... the exotic? I didn't hire... Do
you need anything?

                    LOLA
Music for cleaning. It's all a dance anyway.

He leaves. Lola notices a painting -- a large watchband stretches
across the earth; the moon, stars, and blue sky form the
background. Lola collects dirty glasses and dishes for sink duty.
Charming PIANO melody. She runs the faucet slightly. Michael
returns.

                    LOLA
All these little droplets...

Lola rubs some water on her breasts as she turns toward Michael.

                    LOLA
... it feels so nice to work with my hands.

                    MICHAEL
I don't know what to say. First, you took my
books away, then my thoughts, and... now, my
breath.

                         LOLA
          You make me feel beautiful! Like the belle of
          the ball.

EXT./INT. MICHAEL'S FOYER - DAY

Ongoing MUSIC. Still holding the trophy, Tara opens the door and
progresses into the foyer. Tara proceeds a bit further before
stopping and staring into

THE LIVING ROOM

In disbelief. Michael remains in his robe, but Lola is naked.
She holds a pair of white candles in her hands. Lola and Michael
appear undisturbed by the intruder. An expression of hurt rolls
across Tara's face.

                         TARA
          Of all the sights! How could you, Michael!

Tara sways back down

THE HALLWAY

                         TARA
            Queen takes queen!

And exits slamming the front door behind her!

THE LIVING ROOM

Lola places the candles back in their glass holders on the clock
collection shelf.

                         LOLA
                      (to herself)
          So much garbage.

Lola tickles the clocks with her feather duster. The carved
mirror gets the same treatment.

                              MICHAEL
          Daring move! But now my pawn takes her queen
          and marches on. I just continue to go on some
          sort of magical journey today.

Lola gazes into the mirror, feather duster at ease.

                               LOLA
          And I'm finally going where I want to go. Who
          needs to talk anything over?

                              MICHAEL
Right now, I don't know or even care who sent you. I'll just
figure you're an angel.

EXT. 48TH AVENUE - DAY

Tara and trophy careen into the street. A car screeches to a
halt! Tara continues across the sidewalk. She loses her balance
and steps back and forth before veering into the tunnel.

Tara weaves forward inside the darkened passageway; the beach
and ocean form a light crescent on the horizon. Dwayne springs
out of the shadows and takes Tara by surprise.

The cup falls away. He pushes Tara to the ground, pulls the sword
out of its sheath, and readies it at her chest!

                               TARA
          Oh!

                              DWAYNE
          Prepare to die!

The surf POUNDS louder.

                               TARA
          I'm not scared, asshole!

Dwayne glances at the trophy and spots the inscription.

                    DWAYNE
What! My quest for the grail ends with nothing
but an old British chess cup! This is insane! But
Dwayne still must kill. You could identify me.

                     TARA
Yes... of course, I know you! That's it! And
if you knew who I was, we wouldn't be in this
position. Wake up! It is...
                    (relaxes)

... all revealed. There is nothing other.

Tara in all shivers and smiles as waves of enlightenment
overwhelm her!

                    DWAYNE
Understand something, God damn it! This nightmare
should have stayed in my head. Now, Dwayne will
carry to his death the knowledge that this was
all wrong!

Tara closes her eyes.

EXT. FACADE - TARA'S DAYDREAM

WHISTLING wind. Journey up a rocky wall. Its ledge contains a
brass sculpture of Shakti in all her multi-armed glory.

                   TARA (V.O.)
Enlightenment - now-- Inclusion.

                                            DISSOLVE TO:

INT. QUENTIN AND JUNE'S KITCHEN - DAY

Quentin, mouth twitching, taps a chewed-up pencil. He is table-
side, hunched over a half-solved crossword puzzle. June paces.

                     JUNE
This silent treatment is driving me mad, Quentin.
Are you after some world record? Tell you what.

June picks up a dark bird-shaped jar from the counter, admires it, then throws the jar onto the linoleum. It shatters: Numerous pieces of ceramic and dozens of coins scatter everywhere!

                    JUNE
          I'm going to pay you by the word! C'mon!

Quentin remains silent. June paces around.

                    JUNE
          Look! How about if anything sexual in the
          future involves just the two of us? I only want
          to be with you.

Quentin rises, facing June.

                    QUENTIN
          That's all I've been asking for. My prayers are
          answered.

                    JUNE
          Let's be that couple again, Quentin.

Quentin and June hug and kiss. They flow together onto the floor where both grab and rub coins all over each other! In the process, they yank down each other's pants and underwear.

                    JUNE
                  (ongoing)
          Ooh! Hot! So hot! Yes!

EXT. SAN FRANCISCO - OCEAN BEACH - DAY

The chess cup and sword's sheath on the sand. VOICE OVER occurs while Tara, with an occasional wobble, demonstrates fancy swordplay. Dwayne, his overcoat unbuttoned, gazes on as do a few beach goers.

                    FATHER (V.O.)
          Every piece in chess is more powerful than
          the single pawn. Yet it is only this meek
          single pawn which possesses the supreme power
          of transformation.

Tara makes a few final flourishes with the sword before she thrusts it into the sand.

                         TARA
          Universal body.

Sunlight flashes. She whirls around.

TARA'S POV - BEACH SCENE

A full circle finds ocean surroundings and the beach goers.

Tara's hand grabs the sword to stroke the sand; Dwayne approaches.

                         DWAYNE
          You're certainly advanced beyond my piddly study
          of fencing. Some natural ability?

The sharp blade rises toward Dwayne. He doesn't flinch.

                         TARA
          Magic.

RETURN TO SCENE

Dwayne and Tara face each other. The sword remains pointed at him.

                         DWAYNE
          But, of course!

Dwayne drops to one knee.

                         DWAYNE
          I hope one day you'll forgive Dwayne. I'm very
          thankful he changed his mind before it went
          any farther.

                         TARA
          Forgive and ye shall be forgiven.

Tara brings the sword to her side. Dwayne rises.

                              DWAYNE
          Please make sure that the saber gets returned to
          its rightful owner with my sincerest apologies.

Dwayne drifts away from the beach. Pointed toward his body, the
dart in Dwayne's hand is pure menace as he keeps moving it up
and down!

                              DWAYNE
          Punishment time for getting fuckin' nowhere! The
          sword didn't bring Dwayne the holy grail. There
          was no perfect waterfall, no ultimate garden,
          no doves carrying our daily bread. Everything
          is working out just the opposite. Wait a second!

INT. MICHAEL'S BEDROOM - NIGHT

Michael, wearing boxer shorts and his watch, sits on the edge
of his bed. He turns his nightstand light off.

EXT. NORTH BEACH - NIGHT - MICHAEL'S DREAM

The lights on Broadway illuminate the busy area. Several signs
prove the "UNDRESSED GIRLS" thematic.

INT. DOCTOR'S OFFICE - DAY - MICHAEL'S DREAM

The office contains a gynecological table and a couch. Michael,
wearing a white robe, peers in from behind a room window facing
the table.

An array of sparks parades above the gynecological table. Garbed
in a black slip and black bra, Madeleine perches sideways on
the structure.

                            MADELEINE
          Your choice, Michael. What will it be?

                             MICHAEL
          Hide and seek.

                            MADELEINE
          All three felt different inside me.

                         MICHAEL
          The usual questions.

                         MADELEINE
          Naughty boy.

In profile, Madeleine gets into the stirrups.

                         MADELEINE
          In control.

INT. PET STORE - DAY - MICHAEL'S DREAM

Caged birds, caged dogs. A mixture of CHIRPING and barking.

INT. DOCTOR'S OFFICE - DAY - MICHAEL'S DREAM

Michael still behind the window. Madeleine in the stirrups.

                         MADELEINE
          Embarrass you.

Vacant table. In profile, Michael mounts and puts his feet in
the stirrups. Madeleine smiles from behind the window.

                         MICHAEL
          How did I lose the moment?

Madeleine inhabits the couch.

                         MADELEINE
          Was there ever a moment to lose?

Michael occupies the otherwise empty couch. Madeleine faces out
from a room corner.

                         MADELEINE
          A king, a knight, and a bishop.

INT. PET STORE - DAY - MICHAEL'S DREAM

BUBBLING water. Fish in a tank swim left to right.

INT. DOCTOR'S OFFICE - DAY - MICHAEL'S DREAM

BUBBLING water. On the sofa, Michael, his robe now tattered, and
Madeleine, in a torn dress, gaze at each other.

                    MADELEINE
          The sounds feel so warm.

Michael pulls Madeleine to him, and they kiss.

                    MICHAEL
          Keep telling me the truth.

                    MADELEINE
          You're selfish.

                    MICHAEL
          No; yes! I wish this dream would continue when
          I wake up, Madeleine.

                    MADELEINE
                    (hopeful)
          Are you sure?

EXT. OUTDOORS - DAY - MICHAEL'S DREAM

A flock of birds fly right to left.

                                        DISSOLVE TO:

INT. HOTEL - WESLEY'S PENTHOUSE - DAY

A large well-appointed room is host to scattered comic books
plus a seated Wesley and Tara.

                    WESLEY
          We were having a nice conversation, until you
          turned that on. I warned you the first time,
          politely.

Michael is pointing the camera at Wesley.

MICHAEL
You can't keep exploiting us; it's time to deliver what you promised.

WESLEY
The publicity you and Tara will get -- that alone makes this film worth doing.

Return to the room view with Wesley and Tara.

WESLEY
But, yes, I expect the investors to come through soon with money for the cast, plus your writing fees.

Tara stands to face Wesley.

TARA
Bullshit! We're looking for payment now. Soon is no longer a viable answer, Wesley.

WESLEY
I'd say you got one smart ass in those panties. So, I'll provide a viable answer. Pay attention.

Wesley leaves the room through an inside doorway. He talks while taking a LEAK.

WESLEY (O.S.)
Here's the money stream; look -- pure gold!
(laughs)

You fucking artists never get it; just being involved in a movie with me is pure privilege.

A zipping-up Wesley reappears at the doorway.

WESLEY
I will give you this. I can't wait to see your new powerful climax. You can take that to the bank!

EXT. YERBA BUENA GARDENS - DAY

A five-foot long French bread sandwich rests on a portable table; Tara finishes slicing the loaf into individual portions. Quentin provides food and napkins to a couple of transients.

> QUENTIN
> We do the Lord's work when we help those less fortunate.

A bedraggled man stops by and helps himself.

> TARA
> I honor my father as I feed my universal Self.

The ragged man moseys on, mouth in gear on the sandwich.

> QUENTIN
> That sounds like your personal version of love thy neighbor as thyself. You'll be happy to know it was one of Jesus' favorite commandments.

> TARA
> Interesting. I'm flooded by this feeling of unity. What's going on inside and outside me have found equal status.

> QUENTIN
> And I'm flooded by the feeling that what you just said didn't make any sense.

> TARA
> Everyone is surrounded by what could make them feel complete in an instant. Does that make sense?

> QUENTIN
> (tugs at his cross earring)
> Sure... if that instant includes God.

INT. MICHAEL'S LIVING ROOM - NIGHT

Michael wears boxer shorts; Tara has pants on. Her high heel shoes decorate two sides of the chess board. Both players loom over the chess game.

Quick moves: 44 White PxQ Black P-Kt4 45 White PxP Black K-Kt3
46 White P-Q6 Black P-KKt5 47 White R-Q8 Black K-Kt2 48 White
P-Q7 Black RxP 49 White R-Kt8ch.

                         MICHAEL
        Check.

Tara takes off her pants. Only panties hide her full nudity. She
decides on Black KxR and removes the white castle.

                          TARA
        King takes castle.

Michael replies with 50 White P-Q8(Q)ch.

                         MICHAEL
        Check, Tara! I'm turning my pawn into a new
        queen.

He trades his pawn for the white queen.

                          TARA
        Your chess hero, Paul Morphy, would be impressed.

                         MICHAEL
        I keep my guard up against strong opponents.

                          TARA
        I overlooked some simple moves. I haven't played
        my game.

INT. DION'S LIVING ROOM - NIGHT

A light RAIN falls on the windowpanes. PACKAGE opening. The
rack is still missing its sword and sheath. A swarm of candles
lights the room.

With Dion at her side, Lola pulls a velvet pouch and card out
of a slim box. She glances at the greeting.

                          LOLA
        It's from Destiny. "Dream tonight to make it
        happen tomorrow. Instructions enclosed."

                         DION
     Dream what?

Lola lifts the "people catcher" out of its pouch.

                         LOLA
     Let's start small. How about a group vibration
     at your favorite place?

A surprised Dion grabs hold of both the shiny device and Lola's
hand.

                         DION
     That is thoughtful, Lola. However, it works out,
     let's plan this together.

                         LOLA
     Music to my ears.

The copper star presses between them as Dion and Lola kiss.

INT. MICHAEL'S LIVING ROOM - NIGHT

Whoosh of water RUNNING into a tub. Tara, alone beside the chess
game, remains one small garment away from the buff. She stares
at her chess position.

                         TARA
                    (to herself)
     He's got mate quickly.

Tara concedes the contest by pushing over her king. Along the
wall, two identical clocks keep different times.

INT. MICHAEL'S BATHROOM - NIGHT

Michael luxuriates prone in the steamy waters of his ornate
marble bathtub. Still wearing just panties, Tara enters. Michael
sits up and turns to face his chess opponent.

                         TARA
     You expect all your wishes to come true, don't
     you, Michael?

Not steady, she removes her panties and tosses them at Michael. They land on his face, then fall into the water as Michael revolves toward the faucets.

Tara, high heel shoes in hand, returns dreamlike to the bathroom. She proceeds to throw one high heel in front of Michael. A second shoe splashes into the same location.

INT. MICHAEL'S LIVING ROOM - NIGHT

Tara's balance is not perfect as she puts her pants on. She glances in the direction of the bathroom.

                    TARA
          Won't I be crashing this "come as you are"
          party?

                    MICHAEL (O.S.)
          Madeleine sent the telegram to both of us.
          Meanwhile, there's an emergency.

Michael appears towel-bound in

THE HALL.

He carries wet shoes and panties. Tara arrives at his side.

                    MICHAEL
          These won't be dry until morning.

Apparel dropped. Michael kisses Tara as they twirl their way into

THE BEDROOM

where the bed finds instant company. Flesh and passion unite.

                                        DISSOLVE TO:

EXT. GOLDEN GATE PARK - THE BANDSHELL - NIGHT

DION & LOLA'S DREAM

THE BANDSHELL signage. It's host to a full house. On stage, Dion and Quentin sing the last portion of "STORM RIDER." Dion plays the keyboards while Quentin strums the lead guitar. Lola's bass sounds as sensual as her back-up vocals. June drums away like a pro. Song ends.

                    DION
          No one's a bystander. Everyone's a star!

The audience cheers.

EXT. GOLDEN GATE PARK - THE BANDSHELL - DAY

Destiny wears a black gauze dress; a band of vines permeates her hair. Madeleine, carrying a black canvas bag, sports casual attire including, of course, her artist cap.

Destiny and Madeleine shake hands good-bye and walk in opposite directions. Madeleine branches toward, then disappears into the tunnel.

EXT. SAN FRANCISCO - BLUE HERON LAKE - DAY

Destiny takes a stroll under the waterfall. She emerges drenched.

EXT. BANDSHELL TUNNEL - DAY

Madeleine materializes from the other end of the passageway -- tawdry outfit, long black hair, canvas bag in tow. She glides by leaving pure tunnel in her wake.

EXT. BLUE HERON LAKE ABOVE THE WATERFALL - DAY

A city panorama sparkles behind Dwayne and Destiny. The top of the waterfall cascades behind them. Destiny's wet dress clings to her; Dwayne's ruffled shirt stirs in the breeze. He holds a hand mirror.

                    DWAYNE
          I needed to come full cycle, back to the
          beginning. Sharing the same dreams makes Dwayne
          feel... like there is someone.

                    DESTINY
    Maybe, I wasn't meant to meet you until I moved
    on. But move on to where?

                    DWAYNE
    I came across an answer last time after I tossed
    everything ...

Without paying the slightest attention to it, Dwayne flings the
mirror upward. It sticks in a tree branch with blue sky in the
background.

                    DWAYNE
    ... to the fates.

                    DESTINY
    I'm told to settle for looking for the grail
    spiritually.

                    DWAYNE
    No thanks! Someday, Dwayne's going to find that
    treasure cup for real!

                    DESTINY
    Yes!

Destiny places her arms on Dwayne's shoulders.

                    DESTINY
    We're in the hunt together!

Destiny and Dwayne kiss. With little help, Dwayne's shirt and
Destiny's dress drop from their shoulders. In enthusiastic
embrace, they press up against a tree!

                    DESTINY
    This Joker is wild!

INT. MICHAEL'S LIVING ROOM - NIGHT

The message light is flashing. Michael pushes a button on his
phone answering system.

                              WOMAN (V.O.)
              This is the Herbal Center. In response to your
              inquiry, trifolium pratense, commonly known as
              red clover, is a cancer and tumor fighter. It
              contains a powerful antioxidant form of Vitamin
              E that --

Michael yanks the answering machine plug out of the socket!

                              MICHAEL
              No -- stupid machine!

EXT. DESTINY AND MADELEINE'S FRONT PORCH - DAY

Several times in rehearsal, Michael lowers and raises a bouquet
of flowers. He rings the bell; Madeleine answers.

                              MICHAEL
              I... I want to speak to Tara.

                              MADELEINE
              What you said on that merry-go- round was right.
              It is high time we got off this ride. You're too
              low to ride anyway.

                              MICHAEL
              Please let me see Tara.

Madeleine goes back inside; Tara arrives at the doorway. She
carries the personalized voodoo doll. Michael drops the flowers
as he nods in acquiescence.

                              TARA
              You'd be surprised what some people leave behind
              when they move out.

                              MICHAEL
              Behind -- move out?

                              TARA
              Was all this necessary just to win?

                              MICHAEL
             Just to win -- I was it wasn't going -- I can't
             find the sentence!

Madeleine returns with the nude painting of Destiny.

                              MADELEINE
             Take this home.

She hands the canvas to Michael.

                              MADELEINE
             You and your accomplice deserve each other. It
             makes me sick!

The two women place their arms around each other in defiance.

EXT. SAN FRANCISCO - DOWNTOWN STREET - DAY

A male Salvation Army bell ringer clangs away as he stands beside
the contribution bowl. Michael slinks up and deposits an envelope.
He takes off his watch and places it into the container as well.

MALE BELL RINGER

God bless you!

The nude painting leans against a bench. This is also a convenient
place for Michael to bury his head in his hands.

INT. TARA'S ROOM - DAY

Tara answers her CHIMING cell phone. The sword in its sheath is
a new room accessory. She toys with its handle while listening
to the call.

                              TARA
             In my dad's name? All the money? That is so kind
             and generous, Michael… and yes, I'll be there!

INT. MICHAEL'S LIVING ROOM - NIGHT

Newspapers, magazines, and books are scattered everywhere.
Madeleine's nude painting of Destiny rests against a far wall.

With the sheath nearby, Tara strikes patterns in the air with the sword.

                    TARA
                (looks around)
    Cleaning up anything is not in your vocabulary!
    I'll be returning this sword soon. Meanwhile,
    I'm checking out its potential for love and
    peace.

She puts the sword down.

                    TARA
    I wanted to confide something in one person, but
    I didn't know whom. Your enormous contribution
    to charity -- I knew then.

                    MICHAEL
    I'm listening as hard as I can; I should really
    be talking.

                    TARA
    My mind no longer feels trapped. However, my
    personal body could go --

                    MICHAEL
    Stop! I found out: the red clover. I went over
    to Madeleine's to apologize. I'm so ashamed
    and here I was gloating that the mind games
    were driving you to drink. You should never
    forgive me!

                    TARA
    Wrong.

They hug.

                    MICHAEL
    I love you, Tara.

                    TARA
    I love you too, Michael.

They kiss.

                  MICHAEL

No losers.

                  TARA
                (smiles)

Only winners.

Their lips engage again.

                  MICHAEL

This makes the death scene that's always haunted
me, feel so minor.

                  TARA

It's not minor if it's important to you.

                  MICHAEL

We would need to be in another room.

INT. MICHAEL'S BATHROOM - NIGHT

Michael sits in the empty bathtub; Tara stands next to it. Both
are dressed.

                  MICHAEL

Get the Paul Morphy book; it's right there on
the shelf.

Tara thumbs toward the back of the book as a clothed Michael
remains sitting in the tub.

                  TARA

I think I know which part you want read.

                  MICHAEL

I can't always surprise you.

She reaches a certain page.

                              TARA
          "Paul Morphy used superior development to
          overpower his opponents and was considered a
          chess genius for all time! Meanwhile, there was
          this final circumstance."

Michael shuts his eyes and goes prone.

                              TARA
          "Morphy was found dead by his mother in the
          bathtub in her home on July 10, 1884. He was
          only 47. Morphy suffered a stroke while taking
          a cold bath after a long walk on a hot day."

                              MICHAEL
          Enough.

Michael opens his eyes and gets to standing position in the tub.
Tara opens the door.

INT. MICHAEL'S LIVING ROOM - NIGHT

Michael clutches a tall plastic bottle with a pointy top.

                              MICHAEL
          Expensive fuel time, Tara.

          Liquid squirts out, sparing none of the paper
          on the floor. That includes all the newspapers,
          magazines, and books that are scattered
          everywhere.

Tara gets up from the floor.

                              TARA
          It's still wrap night. We've got to make an
          appearance.

                              MICHAEL
          Get the car and meet me at the corner in five
          minutes.

                            TARA
          Will you be needing a ride, Michael?

                          MICHAEL
          Very funny.

Tara leaves.

Sounds of MATCH lighting. Michael tosses it onto the paper
causing an instant inferno! A rising view captures a messy room
on fire.

                                        DISSOLVE TO:

INT. INSURANCE AGENT'S OFFICE - DAY

In a stark office, a burly, business-suited AGENT works at his
desk, punching numbers into his calculator. Seated opposite the
agent, Michael indulges in a lollipop.

                          AGENT
          I can understand; it's quite a trauma to lose
          everything.

                          MICHAEL
          The producer asked each of us if we had houses
          available for the shoot. You know those low
          budget productions.

The Agent continues calculating.

                          AGENT
          Very commonplace. But low budget or not, the
          good news is that they're still required to
          carry plenty of insurance.

                          MICHAEL
          It's some consolation, I guess.

The agent manages various paperwork.

                          AGENT
          At least, all your documentation made it through.

                    MICHAEL
My safe -- I thought it was a waste of money
at the time.

                    AGENT
              (looks over notes)
It says here, Michael, you were one of the
writers on this project.

                    MICHAEL
Yeah, the lead actress and myself. Typical low
budget -- you write it, you act in it; what
don't you do?

                    AGENT
          (comes upon two official documents)
Certificates of authenticity for an ancient
sword and an historic chess set.
              (whistles)

You never think those things are worth this kind of money. But
that's antiques for you.

He goes back to calculating.

                    MICHAEL
Been in the family for hundreds of years; the
prop department wanted to provide fake stuff;
I should have listened.

The agent shuffles through documents.

                    AGENT
And you're quite the fine art collector. There's
six more official appraisals for sculpture and
paintings by --

                    MICHAEL
Up and coming artist. I helped Madeleine land
the part.

                    AGENT
Don't tell me -- more realism?

                    MICHAEL
                    (nods)
Some of her latest work is quite realistic.

                    AGENT
Good. But you would think artists producing
works this expensive could at least title them.

                    MICHAEL
You would think.

The Agent does more calculations.

                    AGENT
Now, if I've added this right, with what you're
going to get from us plus your homeowner's
insurance, you will come out very well... very
well, indeed.

                    MICHAEL
At least, there were no pets around to get hurt.

                    AGENT
Crews are always watching for that.

                    MICHAEL
I'm glad.

Michael exits the office.

INT. INSURANCE AGENT'S OFFICE - DAY

Wesley paces and occasionally slams a rolled up comic against
his free hand. The agent is at his desk.

                    WESLEY
I'm not interested in being made a permanent
laughingstock. I hope to hell you're still
reviewing those insurance claims.

                    AGENT
Still reviewing?

                              WESLEY
          You heard me, desk jockey. All those valuables
          didn't get to that house by a genie. They
          planned it thoroughly.

                              AGENT
          Any history of paranoia in your family?

                              WESLEY
          They shouldn't get a cent!

The agent rises; Wesley stops pacing.

                              AGENT
          Too late, Wesley.

                              WESLEY
                        (glares at agent)
          Well, idiot, you've just paid arsonists for
          plying their trade.

                              AGENT
          We found no evidence of that.

                              WESLEY
          Now, what are my chances of producing another
          movie?

The agent moves to the side of his desk.

                              AGENT
                          (smiles)
          Would that be ass... tronomical? Meanwhile,
          you're going to lose all value on that comic if
          you keep bending it.

Wesley gets "in your face" close.

                              WESLEY
          I'm holding you personally responsible for this
          sting! And guess what? Sting also means prick!

The agent gives Wesley rough treatment to the door!

> WESLEY
> Hey, this is man handling!

> AGENT
> I'll call when I want more opinions from a
> washed-up producer.

INT. SAN FRANCISCO - RESTAURANT - NIGHT

All the cast members reside around a large oval table. They
enjoy spaghetti dinner and conversation. Michael taps his glass
and rises. The noise abates.

> MICHAEL
> We have gathered you here tonight... he pulls a
> bunch of envelopes from his coat pocket.

> MICHAEL
> Here's the checks for everybody!

Destiny stands and lifts a drink to toast; all raise glasses.

> DESTINY
> Here's to your generosity. It's overwhelming!

> MICHAEL
> I don't know, Destiny. The sword and chess set
> were only gathering dust. Gathering cash is
> better any day!

Everyone gets on their feet.

GROUP

Hoorah!

They click glasses all around and imbibe. Michael begins to
circulate the checks. Tara and Madeleine wander to a corner.

> TARA
> I'll miss you. There should always be time for --

Tara and Madeleine hug.

A passionate lip lock follows.

EXT. SAN FRANCISCO AIRPORT - DAY

"SAN FRANCISICO AIRPORT" sign.

INT. AIRPORT - DAY

Michael, Tara, and Madeleine walk as they carry five suitcases total and a duffle bag.

EXT. SAN FRANCISCO AIRPORT - DAY

A jet takes off.

                                                    DISOLVE TO:

EXT. BIRD'S EYE POV - DAY

People and vehicles appear smaller and smaller. Cumulus clouds drift over things. Tara's SONG "MAN FROM SOMEWHERE" plays.

                        <u>THE END</u>

Printed in the United States
by Baker & Taylor Publisher Services